LET'S GROW!

72 GARDENING ADVENTURES
WITH CHILDREN

BY LINDA TILGNER

Photographs by John M. Kuykendall

STOREY COMMUNICATIONS, INC.
POWNAL, VT 05261

Edited by Deborah Burns

Book design by Leslie Morris Noyes Graphic Design

Cover design by Leslie Morris Noyes Graphic Design

Illustrations by Alison Kolesar

Photographs where indicated by Linda Tilgner

Production by Judy Eliason, Cynthia Locklin and Jeffrey Alves

Typesetting by The Best Type & Design on Earth, South Burlington, VT

The name Garden Way Publishing has been licensed to Storey Communications, Inc. by Garden Way, Inc.

First Edition

Printed in the United States by Alpine Press.

First Printing February, 1988

Library of Congress Cataloging-in-Publication Data

Tilgner, Linda, 1937-
Let's grow!

"A Garden Way Publishing book."
Includes index.
1. Children's gardens. 2. Gardening. 3. Botany—Experiments. 4. Handicraft. I. Title. II. Title: Gardening adventures with children.
SB457.T55 1988 635.9'024054 87-45581
ISBN 0-88266-471-9
ISBN 0-88266-470-0 (pbk.)

To my sons Chips and David
and
to my students,
who taught me how excited children are about growing things,
and how much they can discover on their own,
if you give them the opportunity to try.

ACKNOWLEDGMENTS

Thanks to Dorothy Dunn, former Education Director of the Bennington Museum and Peter Matteson Tavern, for letting us make flower arrangements in the Tavern keeping room; Connie and Hank Van Dine, former proprietors of Ash Wood Nursery, for letting us take photographs there; Jim White, Bennington County Forester, for advice about planting Christmas trees, and for leading many trips in the woods with first graders in tow; Jennifer Kimberly of the Soil Conservation Service, for providing information about soils; James Clark, Bennington County Agricultural Extension Agent, for tips on preparing fruits and vegetables for exhibition in a county fair; David Mance, parent and forester, for sharing maple-sugaring processes and spring woods with my class; Nancy Bower, Registered Physical Therapist, for suggestions on gardening with physically disabled children; Judy Adams, consultant for learning-impaired children, for advice on ways to make gardening meaningful to them; the Berkshire Garden Center and the Sterling and Francine Clark Art Institute, for use of their grounds for photographs; Betty Vander Els, horticulturalist and author, who gave use of her land for growing pumpkins with my class, sheep manure for fertilizing them, and good-naturedly allowed many photography sessions in her yard and kitchen; Geri Thompson, advisor to the Junior Garden Club of the Plain Dirt Gardeners, for information about successful projects for youth organizations; parents of young children (many of them present or former pupils)—Colemans, Fairleys, Kevorkians, Lamberts, Newells, Randalls, Wittreichs, and others—for sharing tips on gardening with children, and for giving permission for their children to appear in photographs; and my sons David and Chips, for their candor in telling me what they, as children, did NOT like about gardening, and what they remember as fun.

Special thanks go to John Kuykendall, whose wonderful photographs have made the joys of gardening with children come alive; to Leslie Morris Noyes, Judy Eliason, and staff, for design and layout; and to my editor, Deborah Burns, whose gentle guidance and creative vision have nurtured all who have collaborated in the production of LET'S GROW!

CONTENTS

PROJECT LIST BY AGE GROUP

Photo by Linda Tilgner

INTERMEDIATE PROJECTS

(for eight- to ten-year-olds)

ADVANCED PROJECTS

(for eleven-year-olds and up)

FAMILY AND GROUP PROJECTS

PROJECT LIST BY SEASON

LATE WINTER, EARLY SPRING

SPRING

SPRING TO SUMMER

Anytime for city dwellers

GARDEN SONG

by David Mallett

(Chorus)
Inch by inch, row by row,
Gonna make this garden grow,
All it takes is a rake and a hoe
And a piece of fertile ground.
Inch by inch, row by row,
Someone bless these seeds I sow
Someone warm them from below
'Til the rain comes tumblin' down.

Pullin' weeds and pickin' stones,
Man is made of dreams and bones,
Feel the need to grow my own
'Cause the time is close at hand.
Grain for grain, sun and rain,
Find my way in nature's chain,
Tune my body and my brain
To the music from the land.
(Chorus)

Plant your rows straight and long,
Temper them with prayer and song,
Mother Earth will make you strong
If you give her love and care.
An old crow watching hungrily,
From his perch in yonder tree,
In my garden I'm as free
As that feathered thief up there.
(Chorus)

CHAPTER 1

LET'S GROW!
THE CHILD AND
THE GARDEN

PLANTING

▲ **Caleb, Jared, and the author plant a salad garden. A gardening project can be a hub from which many investigations radiate.**

PERFECTION

▶ **A growing plant fascinates a child. Rachaele opens a pod to discover the plump peas inside.**

Seven-year-old Jamie rushes to a cauliflower plant and gently removes the clothespins that hold its outer leaves together. "See, this one's almost ready!" he exclaims, as we peer at the white head nestled deep within.

A growing plant fascinates a child. It is magical and exciting to discover the tiny embryo inside a bean seed, to watch the explosion of root hairs as a radish seed sprouts, to see that from one pumpkin seed comes a huge orange fruit with hundreds of new seeds inside, to bury an onion-like narcissus bulb in fall and smell its fragrant flower in spring, to search for delicate wildflowers blooming in spring woods, or to plant a small tree and, as years pass, to watch it grow taller than a house.

Capitalize on the kinship between children and plants. Whether you live in city or country, whether or not you have a vegetable or flower garden, whether you're a parent, a grandparent, a caring neighbor or friend, or an adult who works with an organized group of children, you can harness and encourage a child's natural curiosity about how things grow.

Some of my favorite family memories are of my children in the garden: Chips and David hoist zucchini as huge as watermelon. Four-year-old Chips stands in the borrowed pickup truck beside a mound of rocks hauled from the site for the new lawn; rivulets of sweat descend his dirt-caked face. David, age five, inspects three trash cans brimming with goat manure (more precious to Mom than a birthday gift). Eleven-year-old Chips, wearing his father's battered straw hat, drives the lawnmower, the leaf sweeper in tow, while Dad and David feed the gathered leaves to the shredder. I think of the fun we had working together and the sense of accomplishment we shared for a project completed.

Planting a garden is a bit like raising a child. You nourish the plants, give them love and care, and hope they will respond with lush growth.

As your children grow from year to year, you will observe their development in concepts and skills. Two-year-old Sean drops all his radish seeds in one hole and is delighted that they sprout. That the radishes have no room to develop is of no importance to him then, but the next year, he wants to space the seeds correctly. In starting seeds indoors, one of my first graders puts a seed at the bottom of a plastic cup, then fills the cup with soil. Distressed when her seed doesn't sprout,

PERSONALIZING

▲ **David carves his initials in an immature pumpkin.**

she begins to ask questions and compares her method with that of her classmates. You'll find it exciting, as a gardening mentor, to be a party to a child's growth in understanding.

One of the greatest gifts you can give a child is to cultivate a love for the earth through growing things. Nurture a wholeness in the child's view of the natural world and of the garden's place in it. It's not so much what you do but how you do it that is important. Make it fun!

WHY?

Gardening adventures with children provide some wonderful opportunities. Which of these appeal to you?

■ You can practice sneaky nutrition with nibbles right from the garden. Sweet strawberries, delectable peas, nippy parsley, crunchy young snap beans, sun-warm cherry tomatoes, or baby carrots are vitamin-packed when popped from plant to mouth. Your children may learn to eat vegetables they'd otherwise shun.

■ You can share a family activity in sunshine and fresh air. Gardening is healthy, fun, good exercise, inexpensive, and productive.

■ You can help cultivate in your children a love and respect for the land and a responsibility for its stewardship.

■ You can expose your children to the miracles of growth—a seed germinating in moist earth, a fruit forming from a flower, or a wildflower blooming in deep woods.

■ You can instill a sense of the web of things—bees, bugs, butterflies, birds, earthworms, soil, sun, rain, plants, and flowers—interwoven and interdependent, with human beings a part of it all.

■ You can use the garden as a living laboratory to teach children how food is produced, and that it may come from flowers, fruit, seeds, leaves, stems, or roots.

■ You view a gardening project as a hub from which many investigations radiate—record-keeping, mathematics, science, crafts, cooking, poetry, history, and literature.

There are primarily practical reasons, too, for planning joint activities in the garden:

■ You want to keep the children constructively occupied while you tend the flower or vegetable garden.

■ You need help with planting, weeding, harvesting, and processing, or with gathering organic matter to improve soil quality.

■ You can groom older children to take over lawn mowing or gardening chores and watch them enjoy the satisfactions of assuming responsibility.

One disaster years ago convinced me it is much better to include children in gardening projects than to exclude them.

I had sliced strips of sod, rolled them neatly, wrestled them into the wheelbarrow, and lugged them to the patch of dead lawn near the back door. I had prepared the ground, rolled out the sod, filled in the cracks with sifted soil, tamped it, watered it, and retreated to a steamy bath to soak my tired back, only to find, when I emerged, that my toddler sons had decided that was a lovely place to ride their tricycles. The wheels had made deep ruts in the moist earth, and thrust up edges of the sod I'd so carefully leveled.

I exploded, but later realized it was my fault, not theirs. A few minutes spent devising a way they could have helped, or a few minutes working together to set up a barrier, with kind explanations, would have given them a

BURIED TREASURE

▲ **Peter and Andy help their dad dig potatoes. They show him some of the "treasure" they've discovered.**

LEARNING TOGETHER

▲ **Sean and his mom share garden discoveries. One of the greatest gifts you can give a child is to cultivate love for the earth through growing things.**

stake in the success of the transplant, and there would have been no ruts to repair—in the lawn or in our relationship!

HOW?

How do you include children in the garden? They can help in the family plot, or have a tiny flower or vegetable garden of their own. They can help scavenge for organic soil conditioners, help plant trees, or tend a pot on a city terrace. They can discover nature's gardens in a field, forest, or vacant city

lot, or grow plants indoors.

Adults have many ways of sharing gardening with children, as varied as their own interests and life styles.

■ Two-year-old Andy and four-year-old Peter help Carol Newell to plant the garden. "Sometimes the seeds end up in the wrong place, but that's not as important as the fact that they're staying out of trouble," she explains, laughing.

■ In the Coleman family vegetable garden, Jamie and Christie work side by side with their parents, planting, weeding, and harvesting.

■ Jared and Caleb Randall each have a small vegetable patch in a raised bed next to their parents' garden.

■ Betty Vander Els's four children, and friend Tim, who spent summer days with the Vander Els family while his mother worked, each had his or her own little garden in the big garden. Tim recalls, "That was a big deal. It made you feel important."

■ The O'Briens keep honeybees, and their son Justin raises chickens, whose eggs won first prize in a state competition. Justin and his sister Erin sell their family's sweet corn from a small roadside stand.

■ The four White boys have a Christmas tree farm, a natural for children of the county forester.

■ The Wittreichs sugar together in Vermont's "fifth season," producing just enough maple syrup to supply their own needs and to give as gifts to friends.

■ A city family grows vegetables on a balcony, using wooden produce crates as containers for lettuce, radishes, spinach, beets, and beans.

■ Many communities provide organized gardening activities for children. In rural areas, children learn about growing crops and raising animals through membership in a 4-H club. Youth gardening programs are also offered throughout the world by botanic gardens, environmental organizations, and garden clubs.

GUIDELINES

Whatever your style, keep in mind these basics when you garden with children:

■ Children want results. They have limited patience, so choose crops that are easy to grow and quick to germinate. Stay away from tiny seeds with a three-or four-week germination period.

■ Let children grow what they like to eat.

■ Children like to have fun; keep a light approach.

■ Give a child a small space rather than a large one, or a small, defined task that nests within yours.

■ Spend short, frequent periods for garden maintenance, so that children aren't asked to entertain themselves while you're engaged in a marathon in the garden. If you and the children establish a routine, you'll all be happier!

■ Telling a child to go and work in the garden is rarely successful. Working with them makes it fun.

■ Keep safety in mind. Don't leave poisonous substances where young children can reach them. Teach children not to taste plants unless an adult says it is O.K., and not to leave rakes and hoes point-up on the ground.

■ Maintain a casual, encouraging attitude. Expect high enthusiasm at the start, but realize it doesn't always continue through care and harvest (even for adults!).

■ Give guidance when asked, but let the child make the final decisions about what, where, and how to plant in his or her own garden. It's the process, not the product, that counts.

■ Handle failures in the garden as a natural occurrence, a time for exploring plant needs and mysteries, and the vagaries of weather.

■ Stop and "smell the daisies" occasionally. Look at something wondrous, and wonder about it together. You don't have to have all the answers. Take time out for a hug or a sip of lemonade under the shade of a tree, for a snatch of quality time with your child. □

THIS IS FUN!

▲ **Lindsey is happy in the sun and fresh air of a garden.**

Chapter 2

LET'S GROW! GARDENING WITH VERY YOUNG CHILDREN

Face it. There's no foolproof way to occupy infants and toddlers while you're in the garden so that you'll never be interrupted. Young children flit from one activity to another. They want to be where the action is. They want your attention. They don't want a bean plant to take precedence over their needs.

Gardening with very young children is a special challenge with special rewards. There are ways to make them feel a part of it, to nurture a sense of pride and ownership in the garden, and to water the seeds of wonder that already exist. Here are some hints on how to balance your wish to share the marvels of growing and, at the same time, to keep gardening chores under control, with a child's desire to be near you saying, "I can do it, too!"

BABIES IN THE GARDEN

How you handle gardening with a baby depends on your style of parenting. In any case, an infant is not going to be much help with the weeding!

Garden while an infant naps in a carriage in a shady spot outdoors, within sight and earshot of the garden. Pull a piece of mosquito netting over the carriage to keep bugs away.

You may be able to do light gardening chores with an infant in a sling. That doesn't work for everyone. Deirdre Kevorkian says, "Last year, Seth was six months old. He hated the playpen, or confinement in any way, shape, or form, including a sling, and he wanted to be near me. When I picked beans, I squatted down, laid him in my lap, and reached over him to the beans. He could be on his stomach or back, but he was content."

If you feel comfortable about it, sit an infant right in the garden with you, to be as close to the earth and its fragrances as you are. Nurture a sense of harmony with soil, seeds, and plants by

BERRY PICKING

▲ **(TOP) With a bucket tied around his waist, Sean has two hands free for picking blueberries.**

DISCOVERING

▲ **(BOTTOM) While his mom works in the garden, Conor explores its sights, smells, sounds, textures, and tastes.**

fostering these early connections with Mother Earth. Expect a bit of tasting as part of the investigation.

Remember, too, that some plants, such as potato vines and rhubarb leaves, are poisonous (see chart this page). Protect infants from the hazards of ingesting them.

TODDLERS

Once children can walk, they want so much to be a part of things, to imitate grownups. A toddler can push a toy lawnmower while Mom or Dad mows the lawn, or haul a tiny wagon full of shredded bark or compost while you transport a large load.

Their mobility presents new problems in the garden. Not adept at tiptoeing through the tulips, they may unintentionally walk on young plants or cause other damage. A little planning can minimize the "don'ts" for the toddler.

■ Put a fence around the garden, so a youngster can't wander in at will. You can issue a special invitation when you have a job you want to share.

■ As an alternative, include in your garden plan a space for the child, inside the garden fence. Provide a variety of environments to keep your toddler from getting bored. Give him a sand pile to dig in, some trucks, perhaps a wading pool and, in addition, a little bed of his own to plant. It is important always to bring juice or a snack with you to the garden.

■ Plant in raised beds (see p. 42). Then it's easy to tell a toddler to walk in the paths.

■ Even if you don't opt for raised beds,

LIST OF HAZARDOUS PLANTS

HAY FEVER PLANTS

Grasses

Ragweeds

Flowering trees, especially Alnus (Alder) and Quercus (Oaks)

DERMATITIS & SKIN RASHES

Buttercup

Cactus-like Euphorbias

Carrots

Crown of Thorns

Datura

Dill

Fennel

Gas Plant

Iris

Jimson Weed

Lady's-slippers

Nettles

Parsnips

Poinsettia

Poison Hemlock

Poison Ivy

Poison Oak

Poison Sumac

Rock Poppy

Snow-on-the-Mountain

PLANTS THAT HARM WHEN EATEN

Amaryllis

Autumn Crocus

Azalea

Baneberry

Belladonna

Bittersweet

Black Locust

Bleeding Heart

Bloodroot

Boxwood

Burning Bush (Euonymus)

Buttercup

Caladium

Castor Bean

Celastrus

Cherry, Jerusalem

Cherry, Wild Black

Chokecherry

Crocus, Autumn

Daffodil

Daphne

Datura

Delphinium

Dieffenbachia (Dumb Cane)

Digitalis (Foxglove)

English Ivy

Euonymus

False Hellebore

Glory Lily

Golden Chain Tree

Holly

Hyacinth

Jack-in-the-pulpit

Jequirity Pea

Jerusalem Cherry

Jimson Weed

Laburnum

Lantana

Larkspur

Lily-of-the-valley

Lupine

Marijuana

Marsh Marigold

Mayapple

Mistletoe

Monkshood

Morning Glory

Mountain Laurel

Mushrooms, Death Angel (Amanita)

Narcissus

Nightshade

Oleander

Peyote

Philodendron

Poinsettia

Poison Hemlock

Pokeberry

Potato Vines, Sprouts from Tubers, Green Tubers

Privet

Rhododendron

Rhubarb Leaves

Skunk Cabbage

Taxus (hemlock, yew)

Water Hemlock

Wisteria

poison ivy

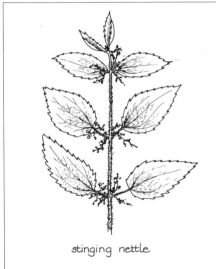

stinging nettle

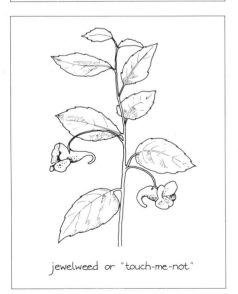

jewelweed or "touch-me-not"

HAZARDS IN THE GARDEN

Every adult who spends time outdoors with a child should be aware that parts of some plants are harmful if eaten and others cause misery (to susceptible persons) if touched. It shouldn't take long to figure out the basic ground rules for safety:

■ Teach a child NEVER to taste any part of a wild or cultivated plant unless an adult says it's O.K. to eat.

■ Teach a child to recognize and avoid touching poison ivy and stinging nettle, two of the most common skin irritants.

POISON IVY
"Leaflets three, let it be." Poison ivy's trademark is its cluster of three leaflets, growing in alternate fashion from the stem. The middle leaflet has a longer stalk than the others. Poison ivy can be a shrub, vine, or trailer. Its leaves can be shiny or dull, smooth or hairy, smooth-edged or toothed, and they turn reddish in autumn. All parts of the plant are "poisonous" at all times of year, even winter. Birds feast on its white berries, so it brings satisfaction to wildlife, if misery to humans. Wash hands and clothes with soap after contact, to keep the oil from spreading.

STINGING NETTLE
Look for opposite, toothed leaves on plants two to four feet tall when you walk along roadsides or in moist woods. These perennial weeds usually grow in large patches. Brush against a plant and say "ouch!" as the hairs on the stems and leaves sting you. Luckily, there's often a jewelweed (or "touch-me-not") nearby. Grab it and rub the juice from its stem on the nettle sting for instant relief.

■ Put "Mr. Yuk" stickers on garden fertilizers and other poisonous substances, and store them out of the reach of young children.

■ Eat rhubarb stalks, but beware of the leaves. They're poisonous. So are potato vines, daffodil bulbs, sweet pea seeds, and parts of many other plants (see list p. 10).

■ Beware of the poisonous coating on treated seeds and some pressure-treated wood, and don't let children nibble on either.

put in a network of pathways, eighteen inches to two feet wide, and mulch them to keep shoes from getting caked with mud.

■ A very young child will make some mistakes in where she walks. Plant a little extra of everything. Then you have some latitude in case a few plants get trampled.

■ Leave a spot in or near the garden where it's O.K. for tots to dig. They like using tools to do the same thing adults are doing, especially if they have their own child-sized ones. But don't be surprised if contentment is shortlived. After a while, they'll probably want to work right next to you.

■ Locate crops that require extra time for harvesting near the edge of the

LITTLE ONES

▲ **Gardens come and go, but your children are only small once.**

garden. Deirdre Kevorkian has done this with her green beans. While she picks (from the outside), Seth, now eighteen months old, can wander around *near* Mom but *outside* the garden.

■ If you plant with your toddler, she'll have a strong sense of where not to walk. ("When Sean's friend Aaron came to visit in the garden it could have been disastrous," says Deborah Burns, "except that Sean told Aaron very sternly where and where not to walk, having helped plant the raised beds.")

PLANTING TOGETHER

Toddlers love to plant things. Flowering bulbs or onion sets are particularly suitable for a two-year-old's developing fine motor control. Point out the top of the bulb and the bottom, where roots will grow, and show where to set it in the earth. Covering it with soil is fun, too.

Choose large seeds, like peas, beans, squash, or radishes, for chubby fingers to drop in a hole or furrow.

"My son Sean loves planting," says Deborah Burns. "The problem is he sometimes puts all his seeds into the same hole. I let the radishes stay there. They all came up in a clump. That was 'his' garden, 'his' patch of radishes. We let them go to seed so we could watch the flowers develop.

"We praise Sean's green thumb. Everything he planted came up, even though it might have been planted in a strange way. I think little children have a special spiritual connection with the earth."

HARVESTING

Picking and eating—that's like a party. When children are really young, letting them pick can be chancy, unless you're able to give one-on-one guidance or

EATING

▲ **Sean picks and eats peas on the outside of the garden fence while his mom works inside.**

there's little possibility for error.

Two-year-old Sean McHugh picks and opens peas that hang on the outside of the garden fence. "He eats while I work inside the fence," says his mom. "It occupies him for quite a while."

When there are two or three young children, it's not as easy to supervise their participation in the harvest. When Lisa, Sean, and Scott Fairley were younger, they held the basket for Mom while she picked. "They were willing for a little while, but it was minimally successful," she recalls, "because soon they wanted to be able to pick, too."

Carol Newell says, "I always find

that getting the kids involved is more effective than trying to divert them from what I am doing." She says that picking in small batches works for her. Andy, Peter, and Lindsay, ages two, four, and six, sit next to the garden on the other side of the pea fence. They shuck while Mom picks. "It's like a game," she explains. "They try to finish shelling one batch of peas before I get there with another."

DIVERSIONS

Every gardener with very young children needs to create some gardenside

WATERING

▲ **Sean waters young seedlings. The raised bed keeps him from walking in the garden.**

activities that will keep children content even though they're not helping.

■ Put a swing set or a sandbox near the garden, preferably in the shade.

■ Set up a wading pool next to the garden, with a beach umbrella for protection from hot sun. Fill it with the same hose you use for watering the garden. The child can watch you garden while she splashes in the pool, and you can talk with each other. Empty the pool water into a dry part of the garden when you're done.

■ Turn on the sprinkler and let tots play in it while you weed.

■ Set up a project right outside the garden. Carol Newell's three children use crayons to create a big mural on a huge cardboard box spread out flat on the lawn, while she catches up on garden chores.

■ Be sure to have snacks available! Shenna and Seth Kevorkian have a picnic while their mom gardens. She gives them small bottles of fruit juice and a carry-out lunch. "It's like a special treat. They sit by the garden. I work; we can talk; they can eat," explains Deirdre.

■ Be willing to take "a stitch in time to save nine" with toddlers. "I tend to keep wanting to work, not stop," says Carol Newell, "but it's really worth it to take a little time off and read the children a story, so they'll settle down contentedly for naps."

ALONE TIME

Use some ingenuity to snatch a bit of solo time in the garden. Team up with a spouse or friend and let one entertain the children while the other works in the garden, and vice versa. Save some gardening chores for long summer evenings, after small children have been put to bed.

Remember, you may need the garden as an escape from the constant demands of loved and active young children. How soothing it was for me, at day's end when Dad took over child care, to withdraw to the side garden and dig among the orange lilies, which glowed with upturned faces from their spot before the fence. The yellow blossoms of Scotch broom waved in the sea breeze and gulls soared overhead in the evening light. It was a peaceful time, a time for renewal.

SATISFACTIONS

The satisfactions of introducing a young child to the wonders of growing surely outweigh the inconveniences.

A child plants a tiny seed and watches a sunflower or a bean pole tepee grow into a giant that towers above him. What a sense of power and awe that creates!

A child comes to regard the garden inhabitants as friends. Sean McHugh's earliest vocabulary included words he learned in the garden—marigold, thyme, peas, squash. He gave guests tours and named each vegetable that grew there.

A child takes pride in growing "all by herself." Shenna Kevorkian, three and a half, has her own little three-foot by five-foot garden, mulched with grass clippings, just like her parents. She has little things she can pick while Mom picks: one cherry tomato plant, a three-foot row of beets, and five green bean plants. "It's all she can handle," says her mom. "She's very proud of it. She washes her own green beans, cuts them up for salads, sighs, and says to her dad, 'I'm such a big girl!'"

Deirdre Kevorkian reflects on gardening with very young children. "What's helped me is to realize you're always going to have a garden. Gardens come and go, but your children are only small once. Enjoy them." □

RIGHT AT HOME

▲ **Conor likes to sit right in the garden.**

CHAPTER 3

LET'S GROW! GARDENING WITH CHILDREN WITH SPECIAL NEEDS

THE PHYSICALLY DISABLED CHILD

A child may have a general physical disability caused by neurological or orthopedic problems, may exhibit developmental delay, or may be visually or hearing impaired. A little ingenuity can make the garden accessible to these children. Help them experience the joy of growing by adjusting the garden to accommodate their special needs.

General physical disability
A disability caused by neurological or orthopedic problems may require a child to be in a wheelchair or to use a walker or crutches. If your child is confined to a wheelchair, bring part of the garden up to his level.

■ Raise a bed. Eighteen inches is a good height for the wheelchair-bound. Construct a frame with landscaping boards and fill it with a friable mixture of topsoil and compost, peat moss, or well-rotted manure.

■ Try a tub. A half-barrel or a ceramic crock filled with easy-to-grow flowers or vegetables can be a disabled child's special growing project.

■ Windowboxes, please. They are the right height for easy care from a chair. Fill them with flower duos, such as dwarf marigolds and ageratum, or geraniums and lobelia. Lettuce, radishes, and garden cress are windowbox candidates—or plant fragrant herbs to snip for kitchen use.

At the Berkshire Garden Center in Stockbridge, Massachusetts, weathered wooden windowboxes set on two-foot-high benches line both sides of a wooden ramp covered with chicken wire (for traction). Narrow boards lift each box off its bench to allow for drainage and air circulation underneath. The boxes are filled with a wonderful assortment of herbs.

GREEN THUMB

▲ **Heather tends an assortment of potted plants.**

RAMP

▶ **At the Berkshire Garden Center in Stockbridge, Mass. windowboxes filled with herbs flank a ramp covered with chicken wire, to provide traction for wheelchair gardeners.**

ACCESSIBLE

▶**(RIGHT) A tabletop plant is the right height for Heather.**

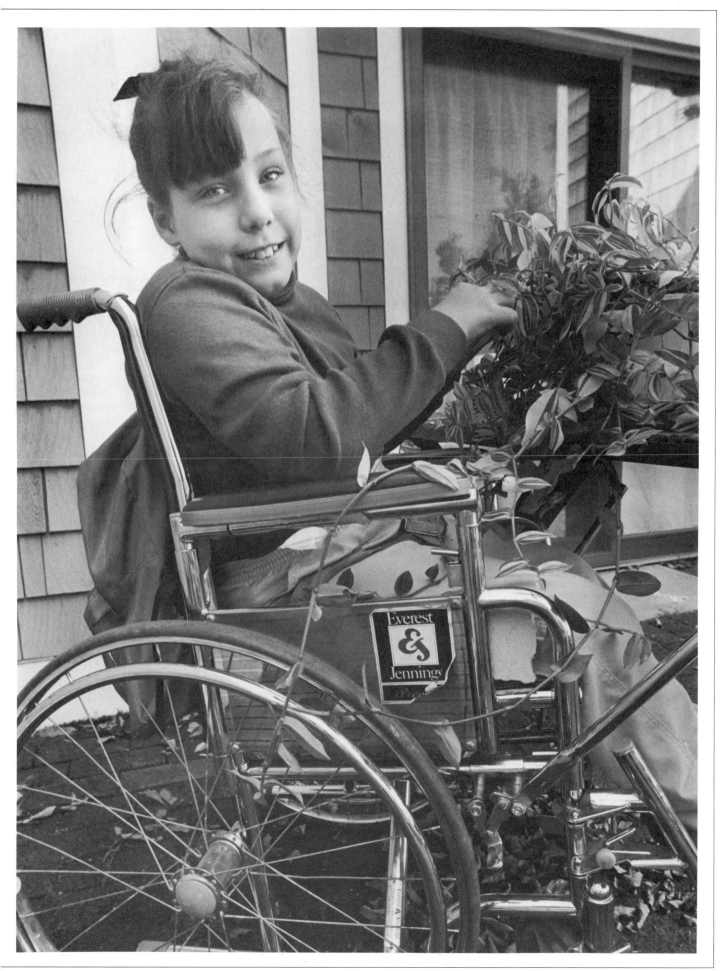

ing chores, with shared responsibility for shucking peas, snapping beans, or husking corn. Many indoor gardening projects are easily adaptable for a physically disabled child.

Development delay
A child may be delayed in developing physical skills. He may talk late, walk late, and learn to do physical tasks later than the average child. Up to five or six years old, his physical abilities and manual dexterity are similar to a younger child's. Give him large seeds and keep everything simple. He might enjoy having his own little patch of garden or his own plant in a pot. (See Chapter 2, "Gardening with Very Young Children.")

The visually impaired
Tailor a garden for the visually impaired child to encourage use of senses other than sight. Focus on textures, scents, and sounds.

■ Clearly define garden boundaries by utilizing raised beds framed with treated lumber or brick. Identify walks with a contrasting texture underfoot. Place a sculpture in the garden for sensitive fingers to explore.

■ A visually impaired child will need a lot of help in planting a garden. Let her identify distinctive seeds by feel—how a corn seed differs from a pea seed, for instance.

■ Grow plants with interesting textures. The large leaves of lamb's ears are soft and fuzzy; the tiny leaves of wooly thyme hug the ground; the feathery foliage of artemesia silver mound or the common carrot tickles as you stroke it.

■ Plant herbs, and encourage the child to crush the foliage to release the distinctive aromas of mint, tansy, catnip, and rosemary. Plant a fragrance garden (see page 103), and share the perfume of the flowers.

■ Atop a table. A table garden is like a giant windowbox set on a table, or on a frame of lumber. Fill it with salad vegetables, herbs, or easy-to-grow annual flowers.

If a child can get around with a walker or crutches, you can prop her up, with the aid of secure seating, right in the garden on the soil. Make a "corner sitter" out of a sturdy cardboard box cut in half, to provide support for the child's back and sides.

The child's hand dexterity may be limited, so choose big seeds—peas, beans, and squash—or use flower or vegetable seedlings. "Skip the carrots," advises Nancy Bower, a registered physical therapist. "Any child under twelve needs an immediate reward, something that germinates fast. That's particularly true for disabled children. Like the rest of us, they think planting and picking are a lot more fun than weeding."

Include the child in food-process-

SUPPORT

▲ **A corner sitter provides secure seating for a physically disabled child.**

▶ **A braille marker identifies purple sage for the visually impaired.**

■ If the child can read braille, use a braille writer to label plants in the child's garden and your own.

■ Add a bird bath to entice birds to the garden. Listen for the sounds of splashing on a warm summer day. Help a child identify the whistle of a cardinal, the joyful conversation of a chickadee, and the meow-like call of a catbird.

■ Lie in cool grass, feel warm sun overhead, smell the fragrant earth, and hear the hum of insects and a cricket's chirp.

The hearing impaired
Except for the loss of pleasure from bird call, breeze whispers, and pattering rain, being hearing impaired is not a handicap in the garden.

THE LEARNING-IMPAIRED CHILD

Because gardening is a hands-on learning experience, it's a wonderful activity for learning-impaired children, especially if not much reading is involved. It is also a way to include these children in a shared activity with family members or with other children.

The adult who works with the learning impaired must be aware of the child's developmental age. Chronologically, the child might be twelve, but his understanding level might be closer to that of a four-year-old. Activities should be appropriate for the developmental level of the child.

A gardening project should be simple enough for the learning impaired to follow through relatively independently. It is important for her to see the entire progression: to plant, to tend regularly, to pick the food, to cut it up in preparation for cooking, to watch it cook, and to eat it. She can't visualize what comes next or imagine the whole cycle unless she experiences it.

"A learning-impaired child has a learning style different from the normal

SILKY-SOFT

▲ **The large leaves of lamb's ears (Stachys byzantia) invite touching and provide a soft texture for sensitive fingers to explore.**

CONVENIENT

▲ **Heather can easily reach this tabletop plant.**

"Whatever you do with a physically disabled child, don't be a perfectionist," advises Nancy Bower. *"Relax and enjoy the garden with them. That's true for any child!"*

child's," says Judy Adams, a consultant for children with these special needs. "Most children learn by 'osmosis'—just by being around someone who is gardening, they will learn a lot. Generally, a learning-impaired child will not grasp a concept from normal exposure. It must be directly taught."

To reinforce the growing cycle and use it as a learning experience, have the child draw a picture each time he does something in the garden: He gets the soil ready, he plants the seed, the plant grows three inches tall, the plant grows seven inches tall, he weeds the garden, and so on. Afterward, talk about each part of the cycle, using the pictures as reminders. Ask the child to sequence the pictures. Add a sentence to the bottom of each to make a story.

Whatever system the child understands for safety should be used in the garden as well. "Mr. Yuk" stickers, for instance, denote harmful substances. Teach proper use of tools and where to hang them when finished, as you would for any child.

Judy stresses the importance of giving the learning-impaired child responsibility. "This type of child is so dependent. Adults who work with them must encourage increasing independence. A normal child will say, 'I can do it myself.' A typical child with limited development will continue to let you take the lead unless you give them responsibility. Helping this child to develop a sense of independence is difficult."

Gardening, she says, has the advantage of being something for which she *can* take responsibility, something she can do independently. Even if it's as simple as the responsibility for watering a houseplant, gardening provides a vehicle for sharing with the family something in which the learning-impaired child can take pride and feel ownership. □

CHAPTER 4

LET'S DIG!
TOOLS TO FIT

WHAT TOOLS DOES A CHILD NEED?

A spade or shovel, a hoe, and a rake are a young gardener's three basic tools.

A rectangular-bladed **spade** is most useful for digging in the garden or for edging. Its flat blade is not very good, however, for picking up soil to move from one place to another. A round-pointed, angle-headed **shovel** works better for that task, and it also can be used for digging.

Hoes come in many shapes and sizes. A **digging hoe,** used for chopping up clods of soil, or for pulling soil up around bush beans, is probably the most practical type to buy for a child. Teach a child to use this tool efficiently. She should hold the tool with the blade down, bend her knees, place one foot ahead of the other, and chop into the soil with an up-and-down motion.

Weeding hoes have shallower blades that cut weed roots just below the surface. A special type called a scuffle hoe is pushed along the ground like a shuffleboard cue.

Every child should have a **steel-tined garden rake.** There's fascination and satisfaction in smoothing prepared soil, and pulling aside stones and roots to make a seed bed.

You may want to supplement the basic tools with others. A **trowel** is useful for transplanting seedlings to the garden, or for planting bulbs. A child could share yours, as size and weight are not as much of a problem with small hand tools.

A **three-tined cultivator** aerates soil around plants and dislodges tiny weeds. It comes with either a long handle or as a hand tool. It would be a nice addition for a child whose interest stays with the garden past planting time.

Most children think leaf gathering

Nothing makes a child feel more like a gardener than her own set of sturdy tools. Nothing discourages a child more quickly than a flimsy plastic hoe that breaks in two after a few encounters with stubborn weeds, or a spindly metal spade that bends with the leverage of digging.

It's equally frustrating to struggle with adult tools that are too long to maneuver and too heavy to lift. That's like trying to ski in an older brother's hand-me-down boots that are so big the messages can't get from foot to ski.

Well-made, child-sized tools with hardwood handles and steel heads are not that much more expensive than fragile tools, and they may last many seasons. Think of them as an investment in a child's success and satisfaction.

DIGGING

▲ **David, the author, Chris, and Jamie use shovels and a spading fork in the pumpkin patch.**

CHILD-SIZED

▶ **Sean can choke up on the handle of this sturdy child's shovel, and continue to use it as he grows taller.**

is great fun, at least for the jumping-in-them part of the task. Invest in a sturdy, child-sized **leaf rake** for help, token or real, with this annual job. You may get some aid with spring lawn cleanup, as well.

A child feels important with a **small wheelbarrow,** to help cart materials to the compost pile, move mulch to his own garden, or move soil from one place to another.

Children can share your **watering can,** or you can buy a special one for their use.

An older child might like to have his own supply of **garden stakes, string, markers, tomato cages,** and some **graph paper** for planning garden layouts to scale.

City dwellers whose gardens are in containers on balconies or terraces could outfit a child gardener with a collection of hand tools, a watering can, and a spray-misting bottle.

HOW BIG?

Tools should be approximately shoulder high, anywhere from a little below the shoulder to a foot or so above it (which will allow for the fact that children, like plants, grow!). Kid-sized tools, about three feet high, are designed for children from two to six. Seven- to twelve-year-olds can use the next-larger size, about four feet high, often called lady-sized or patio tools.

Straight handles are preferable to D-handles, as they have more latitude for growth of the user. A short child can choke up on a straight handle to get better leverage.

HOW BRIGHT?

Many children's tools come in a bright color—orange or red—which helps to locate them if they are laid down in the garden or on the lawn. Haven't each of us played needle-in-the-grass with a misplaced tool at least once?

THE RIGHT TOOLS

▲ **Nothing makes a child feel more like a gardener than a set of tools of the right size. Sean and Megan work in the family vegetable garden.**

TEACH SAFETY

Points down, please! Before someone steps barefoot on the sharp tines of a rake, or stumbles on the upturned blade of a hoe and sends the handle whipping toward a vulnerable forehead, stress the importance of leaving rakes, hoes, cultivators, and shovels points down if one must set them aside.

Ask "What will happen if . . . ?" and do a bit of play-acting to show the consequences of carelessly flung tools. Role-playing can be done with humor, and it makes a more lasting impression than admonishment.

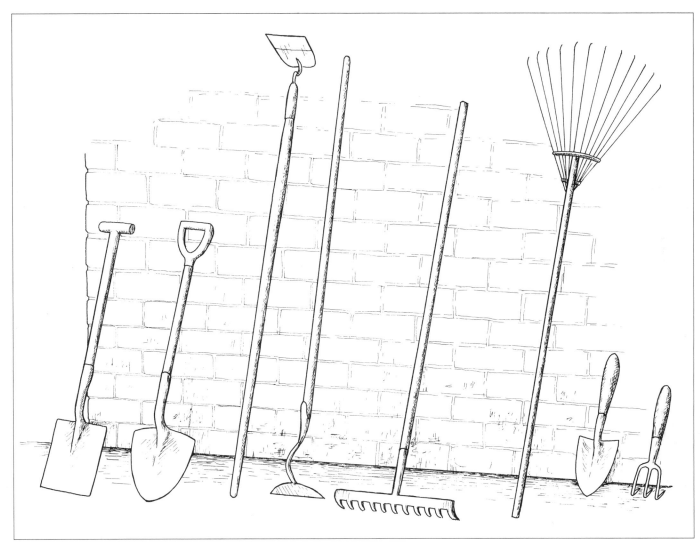

If your tools don't have this splash of brilliance, take a few minutes to paint a band of fire-engine color (with enamel paint, to resist weather) on the handles of gardening tools that belong to you and the child. Work together to sand the surface lightly and wipe it down with turpentine before painting.

A PLACE TO DIG

When you provide a child with a special set of tools, be sure to set aside a space where he can experiment with them. It could be a dirt pile, a corner of your garden to be planted later in the season, the child's own garden space, or a spot at the edge of your lot. Every

child needs a little "play time" with a new possession.

A PLACE TO HANG

Make a special place for a child's special tools to hang, preferably near yours. To store tools on the garage- or shed wall, nail a piece of pegboard Masonite to the beams, and purchase metal hooks to fit the tools. The advantage to this arrangement is that it can be revised as more tools are added to a child's collection.

For a very young child, paint the outlines of the tools on the Masonite, to show which belongs where. It allows for a quick check at day's end to see if

TOOLS

▲ **left to right: rectangular-bladed spade, angle-headed shovel, digging hoe, weeding hoe, steel-tined garden rake, leaf rake, trowel, three-tined cultivator.**

everything's been put away, or what might still be lost among the pea vines. An older child can make labels for each tool's hook by embossing plastic tapes on a labeling machine or hand lettering labels with permanent markers.

TEACH TOOL CARE

Help a child learn to care for tools. In working side by side with you, the child establishes a lifelong attitude toward maintenance, and develops pride in ownership.

An easy way to clean tools after use and to prevent rust is to keep a bucket of oily sand where tools are stored. Fill a bucket with sharp sand. Add about a quart of motor oil (ask a garage for some used oil), and mix. Each time you're finished using a tool, plunge it into the oily sand a few times. It will remove dirt, and leave a protective coating of oil on the metal.

Hoes and spades do the job well only if they're sharp. Work with your child to secure the head in a vise, and use a file at an angle to sharpen the cutting edge. File at the same angle as the original bevel. Always file a hoe from the outer edge toward the inner edge.

Center the cutting edge of a spade or shovel, and don't file it too thin or it will nick easily.

Winter is a time to refurbish neglected tools. Wire brush rusted metal parts, or rub them with steel wool or emery cloth, then wipe with an oily rag. Sand wooden handles and apply a coat of paste wax. Check that heads are tight in their handles. If not, reinforce with adhesive. If the head is really loose, tap in a couple of shims. □

LEARNING

▲ **Give a child a place to dig.**

▶ **Sharpening a hoe.**

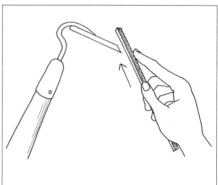

CHAPTER 5

LET'S DIG! SOIL

Photo by Linda Tilgner

SPRINGTIME

▲ **Jared holds a new lamb.**

DIGGING

▶ **Soil rich in organic matter makes easy digging for Rhea.**

Whether you're a child or an adult, the most important ingredient for gardening success is the soil. Fluffy, spongy soil, rich in organic matter, practically ensures good crops. It is easy to spade or hoe, provides the nutrients plants need for lush growth, holds moisture so that frequent watering is unnecessary, and nurtures healthy plants that are resistant to disease and insect attack. Under these conditions, a child's enthusiasm for growing things is likely to blossom along with the plants he nurtures.

How sad, though, for a child to try to grow a garden in unenriched soil of little tilth. She may give up even before the garden is planted, after wrestling with tools that won't push easily into cement-like hardpan.

Plants don't like it much either. If seeds germinate at all, the seedlings are likely to be yellow and stunted and succumb quickly to disease and ravaging insects. Discouragement and frustration are probably all the child will harvest from this garden.

We preach healthy habits to our children: Eat nutritious food, drink plenty of water, breathe fresh air, get plenty of exercise and a good night's sleep; and we give them lots of that invisible ingredient, love.

A child can understand the parallel between human needs and plant needs. Plants, too, need food, water, air, sun, and love. Make this connection, and make a big deal out of soil preparation. Build healthy soil for healthy plants.

HOW?

How do you make soil healthy? Add as much organic matter as you can. Add it directly to the soil by digging or tilling it in; lay it on the soil as mulch, which will gradually decompose; plant a green manure to turn under as organic fertilizer; or make compost to enrich the garden soil.

As you replenish the soil's organic matter on a continuing basis, you expose a child to the idea of natural cycles. You will be imitating in the garden what happens in a forest or field, where leaves or grasses from the previous season are returned to the earth, along with animals that die, to provide food for next year's growth.

SCAVENGING FUN

Scavenging for organic soil builders can be a fun family or group activity. Look for manures, leaves, and non-hazardous, organic wastes from local industry to add texture and tilth to the soil. An expedition to collect these materials often provides a chance for children to learn about the animals or industries that produce the waste.

My class visits a neighborhood sheep farm in the spring. The children delight in watching newborn lambs bounce off the ground as though they were riding pogo sticks, run to take a quick sip of milk from Mother, and bound away again. We feel the lanolin in the ewes' winter coats, and see the sweaters knitted from their wool.

We find lambs' tails on the barn floor, where they've dropped off after being tied with a rubber band, in much the same manner as an infant's umbilical cord. Now we understand why, when Little Bo-Peep found her sheep, ". . . it made her heart bleed, for they'd left their tails behind them."

Later, Paddy, David, Chris, and Jamie gather sheep manure to bury under our pumpkin hills. The hill with the largest dose of manure produces the most vigorous vines and the biggest pumpkin—a vivid "thank you" from the plant.

Manures
Farmers usually use the manure from their animals to enrich their own fields,

▼ **The leaf pile is a place for jumping and burrowing. Allyson and Ryan think this is the best part of leaf gathering.**

WHAT IS SOIL?

Soil is the giver of life to plants, to the animals that eat plants, and to the animals that eat the animals that eat plants. It is the top layer of the earth's surface, made up of minerals from ground-up rock, decomposed plant and animal matter, water, and air. Soil is alive with living organisms, from tiny bacteria you can see only with a microscope to the earthworms that "plow" it, digesting organic matter as they go.

AUTUMN LEAVES

▶ **Raking is only half the fun.**

or charge a high price to deliver a load. Search for friends who raise a few animals as pets or for food. Often, they'll share manure from horses, sheep, goats, pigs, or chickens if you are willing to cart it away.

Pet rabbits, gerbils, hamsters, and birds provide droppings that enrich garden soil. Fur brushed from the coat of the family dog or cat can be dug into a child's garden, to provide nitrogen as it decomposes.

Leaves
What child doesn't love to jump in huge piles of autumn leaves—to burrow under them, hear their crunch and rustle, smell their fragrance—and toss leaves in the air and see them flutter in the wind. You may even get a bit of help with raking them! Then dig them into the garden or add them to the compost pile. They'll decompose faster if you run the rotary lawnmower over them first.

Industrial waste
Explore the availability of free or inexpensive organic industrial waste in your community. Get shredded bark, wood chips, and sawdust from a sawmill; apple pomace from a cider mill; grape pomace from a winery; spent hops from a brewery; cottonseed hulls, wool, felt, or silk wastes from a textile mill; fish scraps from a fish market or commercial fishing party boat; or leather dust from a tannery.

MULCH

Besides making the garden look neater, mulch will smother weeds, and that's a plus for any child, who may not stick to weeding throughout the growing season. It also holds in moisture, keeps soil temperature even, and, as it decomposes, enriches the soil.

Common organic mulching materials are hay; salt hay; straw; shredded sugar cane; wood chips; shredded

MANURE

▲ **Paddy and David dig sheep manure from the barn to enrich the soil for their pumpkins.**

bark; grass clippings; newspapers; shells from grains, beans, or nuts; eelgrass; seaweed; coffee grounds; and pine needles. Most of these mulches are free from weed seeds that may sprout after the mulch is placed around plants. Grass clippings and hay both come from grasses, but because you mow the lawn before grasses go to seed, the clippings won't sprout weeds. Use seed-free clippings in finicky places, such as flower gardens. Hay is a more practical mulch for your vegetable garden. Pile it on thickly and turn it or add more hay if weeds begin to sprout.

Sidedress plants with a high-nitrogen fertilizer before adding mulch for the first time. Pile on the mulch about twice as thick as you think you need it.

GREEN MANURES

The simplest way to demonstrate to a child the use of a green manure is to

dig under pea vines or bean plants directly in place, as soon as the harvest is over (see pp. 56 and 58). Peas and beans are members of the legume family. On their roots are little bumps or "nodules" in which "nitrogen-fixing" bacteria live. These special bacteria take nitrogen from the air and turn it into a form plants can use. When you return legumes to the soil, you're adding extra nitrogen as well as organic matter.

Gardeners sometimes seed a green manure (also called a cover crop) on the entire garden when the harvest is over in the fall, and turn it under in spring. Grains such as winter rye, annual ryegrass, barley, oats, and wheat are often used for this type of soil enrichment.

COMPOST

Let a child help build a compost pile, and, at the same time, strengthen his or

▲ **The author helps Sarah and Chris use a food processor to grind up materials for anaerobic composting.**

WHY DO YOU NEED AIR?

The process of turning raw materials into crumbly compost is carried out by microorganisms called aerobic bacteria. They need air in order to do their job of decomposition. As they turn the carbon in the waste materials into energy, heat is created. Stick an oven thermometer into an active pile and watch it rise as high as 150°F or 160°F! Look for the earthworms that gravitate to the pile after it cools down.

her concept of recycling, as weeds, garden refuse, kitchen scraps, leaves, and other organic materials lose their identity and become the black fluff of new soil.

You can make compost in layers (three parts green matter, one part manure, and a bit of soil) or in a casual pile. Put it in concrete block or fenced three-sided bins near the garden, or in a wire cylinder about three feet in diameter placed right in the center of the garden, where it will be a handy depository for garden, lawn, and kitchen refuse, plus an occasional shovelful of soil.

Train your children to put banana peels, apple cores, peach pits, citrus skins, carrot tops, egg shells, and the like into a half-gallon milk carton kept near the kitchen sink. Add its contents to the compost pile (or tuck it under garden mulch).

Keep the pile moist but not sodden and make sure there are plenty of air spaces within it. Tom Coleman says, "The main thing a compost pile needs is air. I add it the easy way, by periodically running the rototiller through it. My compost is ready to use in two months."

Anaerobic compost
It's also possible to make anaerobic (without air) compost, in which a different kind of bacteria digests the organic matter. Theoretically, there is less nutrient loss in this type of composting. Some northern gardeners compost anaerobically in winter, when they can't get to their compost piles through deep snows.

My first graders tried it. On a Friday, the students cut weeds, autumn leaves, vegetable peelings, and fruit rinds into tiny pieces. Our classroom looked like a factory, with twenty pairs of hands busily snipping. We put this organic matter into a plastic garbage bag, along with manure from neighbor-hood sheep and some garden soil, moistened it with water, and fastened the top securely with a twist tie.

On Monday morning, the custodian greeted me. "Linda, I think there's something wrong in your classroom. It smells TERRIBLE in there!"

Sure enough, a horrendous odor was coming from our bag of compost. It showed that the process was working as it should, for unpleasant odor is a characteristic of decomposing anaerobic compost. What is the odor? It's methane gas, a byproduct of this process.

We added a heavier plastic bag to the outside of the first and moved our experiment outdoors. Our pumpkin vines grew vigorously when we buried the compost under the soil, but we would recommend anaerobic compost-making with children only if you like vile smells!

LEARNING MORE

The simplicity and necessity of returning organic matter to the earth is the important message to give your child through shared activities in soil enrichment.

If either of you has an interest in such things, you can demonstrate the benefits of soil enrichment by planting the same seeds in two environments: enriched soil high in organic matter, and sand or clay with little tilth. See if there's a difference in how the plants grow.

Acid or alkaline?
You and the child can investigate the acidity or alkalinity of soils. Buy a simple test kit, or send soil samples to your state's agricultural extension service. Their literature will tell you how to take thin slices of soil from several places in the garden and where to send it for testing.

Acidity or alkalinity is stated in pH,

NPK: THE THREE BASICS

Older children might like to learn about the three basic elements needed for plant growth: nitrogen (N), phosphorus (P), and potassium or potash (K). Although it's an over-simplification, you can associate nitrogen with leafy green growth; phosphorus with abundant flowering, necessary for crops which produce fruits, such as tomatoes, peppers, eggplant, peas, beans, and squashes; and potassium with strong stem and root growth.

Organic sources of nitrogen are manures, green manures, fish emulsion, blood meal, cottonseed meal, and alfalfa meal. Bone meal and rock phosphate are high in phosphorus. Wood ashes, greensand, and granite dust provide potassium.

There is a bonus in returning plants to the soil. In addition to the three basic elements—nitrogen, phosphorus, and potassium—they contain many trace minerals needed for plant growth, such as boron, cobalt, copper, iron, manganese, molybdenum, and zinc. Many of these trace minerals have been brought up from deep in the earth by plant roots.

All this "food" is released slowly by organic fertilizers, so you never have to worry about plants getting "indigestion." With chemical fertilizers, you must be careful not to apply too much at once, or you may burn plant roots.

Examine the numbers that indicate NPK ratios on commercial fertilizers to see how they vary according to purpose. Lawn fertilizers, for instance, are much higher in nitrogen (to stimulate green, leafy growth) than are rose fertilizers, which are highest in phosphorus (to stimulate flower production).

on a scale from 0 (very acid) to 14 (very alkaline). Neutral soil has a pH of 7. Keeping soil at the correct pH is important, because nutrients necessary for plant growth become unavailable to them when the pH is too high or too low.

Most plants like a soil that is slightly acid or nearly neutral (a pH of 6 to 7). Some, such as azaleas, blueberries, and potatoes, need an acid soil; and a few, such as clover, alfalfa, and iris, like more lime. You can increase the alkalinity of soil by adding ground limestone or wood ashes, or increase its acidity by incorporating evergreen needles or peat moss, or adding elemental sulfur in measured amounts.

Air and water
Even young children will like to know that plant roots breathe. They take in oxygen and breathe out carbon dioxide, just as we do. The oxygen reaches plant roots from the air, through spaces between soil particles, and the carbon dioxide gets out in the same way. If there's not enough air space in the soil, the roots suffocate. About a quarter of the volume of good soil is air, and organic matter helps to keep those air spaces open. So do earthworms, which seek out soil high in organic matter.

Another quarter of good soil is water. Organic matter helps to keep that in the soil, too. Too much water will literally drown plants, because it fills up all the air spaces so roots can't breathe.

Clay soil is composed of tiny particles that stick together and leave little room for air. Sand is made of large particles with lots of air space, so much that it won't hold water for very long. Loam has the best combination of air, water, organic matter, and minerals for nurturing plant growth.

How is the mineral part of soil made? A budding geologist may be in-

▲ **See what lives in a shovelful of soil!**

MICROSCOPIC MAGICIANS

Plants need nitrogen for growth. Air is 78.1 percent nitrogen, but the nitrogen in air is not directly available to plants. Special bacteria convert the nitrogen from air into nitrogen compounds that can be used by plants. This process is called "fixing." Some of these special nitrogen-fixing bacteria live inside the little bumps or "nodules" on the roots of peas, beans, and other legumes.

PLANTING

▲ **Good soil is crumbly, moist, and loaded with organic matter.**

terested in learning about the role in soil formation of weather, erosion, glaciation, and sedimentation. Visit road cuts to see the story of the earth laid down in layers, back through time.

Soil creatures
Most children, given a choice, would rather look at animals than plants. Take a shovelful of soil from the richest part of your vegetable garden and dump it on an old sheet or a large piece of white paper.

See what lives among the plant roots! A magnifying glass will help you and the child see the intricacies of the smallest creatures. A one-inch-square magnifier box will keep a small, scurrying animal confined while you scrutinize its characteristics before returning it to the garden.

If curiosity is high, compare the type and quantity of soil inhabitants

from different places: from the lawn, from the gravelly edge of the road, from beach sand, from the forest, or from the edge of a pond.

SQUEEZE-A-HANDFUL

One last lesson: In spring, most gardeners, especially young ones, can't wait to begin planting. But you can ruin the soil's structure if you dig in too soon. Teach children the old squeeze-a-handful test to see if soil is dry enough to work. Scoop up a handful of soil, squeeze it, poke it with a finger, and see what happens. If it crumbles, it's ready for planting. If your finger makes an indentation and the soil stays in a lump, it's too wet. Wait a while and try again.

Do you know that an abundance of organic matter will help the soil to dry out earlier in the spring? □

MAKE MANURE TEA

This brew will be a welcome drink for young plants in your garden (but not for you!).

YOU NEED

- A 5-gallon plastic bucket with cover (often available as a castoff from industry)
- Enough manure to fill ¼ of the bucket
- Water

TIME OF YEAR

Spring and summer, when crops are growing

TIME NEEDED

Two weeks

MANURE TEA

▶ **(TOP) Katie and her dad shovel rabbit droppings into a bucket.**

SOURCE

▶ **Sean gives Fluffy water while Katie and Megan watch. Their pet rabbit provides the droppings for manure tea.**

Brew the tea
Put manure in the bucket until it is about ¼ full. Fill the rest of the bucket with water. Cover it. Each day, agitate the bucket. In about two weeks, your "tea" will be ready.

Feed your plants
Dip out some manure tea and drizzle it on the soil next to young seedlings. If it seems very strong, dilute it with a little water. Tomatoes and lettuce will love it. Pumpkin, squash, and cucumber vines will thank you with vigorous growth. So will broccoli and spinach. Use it for any plant that needs a boost of nitrogen.

Replenish the tea
Continue to add water to the same batch of manure until the tea looks pale and weak. Then dump the used manure on your garden or compost pile and start again.

VARIATION

For vegetarian tea rich in potash, use comfrey leaves instead of manure.

TRANSPORTING

▶ **Pushing this load of manure out of the sheep barn is a two-person job. Paddy and David can dig it into the garden or use some to brew manure tea.**

START AN EARTH-WORM COLONY

Earthworms are more than bait for fish! See how these soil friends digest organic and mineral matter and make tunnels in the soil for easier movement of air and water.

YOU NEED

- A large glass container: an aquarium or a gallon wide-mouth jar, with a screen cover or a lid with air holes
- A trowel
- Garden soil
- Compost materials: weeds, autumn leaves, vegetable parings, fruit skins, rotted straw or hay, grass clippings
- Scissors or food processor
- Manure, blood meal, or cottonseed meal
- Water, spray-misting bottle
- Black paper to cover the outside of the container
- Tape or a stapler

TIME OF YEAR

Anytime, but earthworms may be easiest to find in spring and early summer, when they're most abundant

TIME NEEDED

Two to four weeks

Make worm food
Cut the compost materials into small pieces. Use scissors, or if Mom will let you, chop them up in a food processor. Mix with the manure, blood meal, or cottonseed meal.

Make a worm home
Put alternate layers of garden soil and chopped-up worm food in the glass container. Sprinkle a little water on each layer so it is moist but not soggy. Leave a couple of inches of space at the top. Let it sit for a few days. Stir occasionally, and sprinkle with water to keep moist.

Go worm hunting
The best time to find worms is at night or after a rain, when they are close to the surface. Do you have a friend who likes to fish? Bet she can help you find some nightcrawlers! Put a bunch of worms on top of the soil in the worm home. Watch them burrow into the earth.

Give them privacy
Cover the outside of the container with dark paper, so the worms will venture close to the glass. Lift off the paper only when you want to observe the worms. Cover the top of the container with a screen or a lid with holes punched in it.

Worm care
Keep your worm home in a shady place. Worms do not like sun or heat. Keep the soil moist, and add snipped-up organic matter from time to time. See if your worm population grows!

Look, look, look
When you lift off the paper, can you see the worm tunnels? In your garden, these help plant roots to get air, and rain water to run into, not off, the soil. Look for castings—little piles or oval masses of fine soil that has been digested by the worms. These castings provide food for plants.

Take out an earthworm. Use a magnifying glass to look for the little hairs, called setae, on the underside of the worm. Watch how it uses its muscles and the setae to move. Count the segments. The worm's mouth is behind the first segment, on the underside.

Did you know?
- that there are more than 3,000 kinds of worms in the world?
- that a single earthworm can produce its weight in castings in one day?
- that earthworms can live only in soil that has abundant organic matter?
- that many earthworms die in the hot, dry heat of summer, and their decaying bodies provide MORE food for plants?
- that you can prevent some death from summer heat by mulching your garden?

ARE EARTHWORMS HELPING YOUR GARDEN?

To find out, cut out a one-foot square of soil seven inches deep and count the earthworms in it. If you have at least ten, earthworms are helping to give your crops air, water, and nutrients.

See also Chapter 9, "Garden Helpers."

A LONG ONE

▶ **David examines a nightcrawler.**

CHAPTER 6

LET'S PLANT! VEGETABLES

CONCENTRATION

▲ **Tadhg is completely absorbed in planting hills of corn, pole beans, and squash.**

LET'S GET STARTED

▶ **Lindsey carries pepper seedlings to the garden.**

Vegetable growing is particular fun for children, because it results in a product of obvious value—food to eat. Often, the most active years in the vegetable garden are those in which a young family is forming and growing. Interest in home and garden is high, and working together in sun and fresh air is inexpensive family recreation.

PLAN FIRST

Decide how you can best include children in your own gardening activities. You may share the chores in the family garden with them; give each child a corner, a bed, or a row in the main garden; or a separate patch next to yours. However you structure their participation in vegetable growing, make sure they're right near the center of activity. They need to feel important and a part of things. That's what makes their experience a sucess.

THE SITE

The same guidelines for locating a vegetable patch apply to either a child's garden or your own:

■ *Vegetables need sun,* at least eight hours a day. Keep the garden away from the shade of buildings and trees. Locate tall crops on the north side of the garden, where they won't shade out shorter ones.

■ *Vegetables need water.* The garden should be as close to a hose or outdoor faucet as possible.

■ *Vegetables need food and good soil structure.* Spend lots of time loading up the garden with organic wastes (see Chapter 5). Locate the compost pile nearby, and situate the garden away from trees and shrubs, whose roots will steal nutrients from crops.

■ *Vegetables need good drainage.* A gentle tilt to the south (for sun and warmth) is ideal. In any case, avoid precipices and ravines.

■ *Vegetables need to be picked regularly.* Place the garden as close to the kitchen door as you can.

■ *Vegetables need protection* from marauders. If your garden needs a fence to discourage nibbling rabbits and woodchucks, the child's garden does, too.

ABRACADABRA— SOD BECOMES SOIL!

If you're giving a child a plot of her own, you can avoid the backache of digging up sod if you plan ahead. Lay out the size and location of the young gardener's patch in the fall, or a couple of months before planting time. Cover it completely with a thick layer of newspapers, cardboard boxes opened flat, or a piece of black plastic. Weigh down the covering with a layer of shredded bark, stones, or a few pieces of scrap lumber.

RAISED BEDS

Start with a well-prepared seedbed. Enrich it with compost, manure, other organic matter, and/or fertilizer. Form the raised beds with either hand tools or a tiller with a hilling attachment.

Keep it simple with hand tools:

1. Mark the bed with stakes and strings. Make them 18 inches to 3 or 4 feet wide and any convenient length. Walkways can be up to 20 inches wide. (One gardener makes them the width of a bale of hay for efficient mulching of walks.)

2. Use a rake to pull soil from walkway to the top of the bed. Stand in one walkway and draw soil toward you from the opposite walkway. When you have completed one side, repeat the process from the other side.

3. Level the top of the bed with the back of the rake. Sides should slope at a 45-degree angle. A lip of soil around the top edge of a new bed will help reduce erosion.

Help from a tiller:

1. Stake out walkways of two tiller widths.

2. Attach furrowing and hilling attachment to the tiller. Set hilling wings to the highest position, so they will push soil upward onto the bed.

3. Hill up beds. Line up the center of the tiller in front of the first stake, point it at the stake at the other end of the bed, and guide tiller directly toward it. Repeat on the other side.

4. Smooth the top of the bed with a rake.

To plant raised beds, broadcast small seeds as you would for a wide row. Larger seeds (such as for bush beans or transplants such as cabbage) should be spaced the distances recommended for a conventional row, but the spacing should be in a pattern that lets the leaves of mature plants barely touch one another, providing a living mulch.

MAKING RAISED BEDS BY HAND

▲ **Step 1. Mark the bed with stakes and strings. Pull up soil to make a raised bed.**

Step 2. Level the top of the bed with a rake.

FASTER WAY

▶ **Use a tiller to push up the soil for raised beds.**

STEP 1

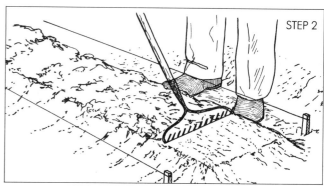

STEP 2

The grasses and weeds underneath, deprived of sun, will die, decompose, and enrich the garden patch. When it's time to prepare for planting, the newspapers or cardboard may be soft enough to dig right into the soil. If you used black plastic, just lift it to find easy digging.

THE LAYOUT: BEDS AND PATHS

Many families with young children find that raised beds (from eighteen inches to three or four feet wide) with well-defined paths between them work best. Then nobody ever stomps where plants are growing, compacting soil and squishing seedlings. The crops are also less vulnerable to trampling by an enthusiastic retriever of an errant frisbee or baseball.

Weeding, watering, cultivating, and harvesting are all done from the pathways—easy for a youngster to manage without stumbling over fragile crops, as he might in a traditional row garden.

Keep the paths weed-free with mulch—"books" peeled from hay bales, straw, grass clippings, shredded bark, pebbles, or the like. Underlay the mulch with plastic or thick pads of newspaper as further protection from weeds. Or put mowed grass paths between the beds, instead.

WHAT TO PLANT?

When seed catalogs arrive, let the children help make choices, either for your garden or their own. Older children might be able to plan their gardens on graph paper, with a little adult help.

Tom Coleman thinks it's important to have variety in the family garden. "This year the youngsters are interested in one thing; next year it will be something else. Last year, Jamie's rage was peas. This year it's carrots. Christie is into fruits—raspberries and strawberries. Parents shouldn't reject a child's

IDEAL

▼ **A good garden site has sun at least eight hours a day.**

interest. Don't try to steer them into something else."

Choose favorites
Do grow what children like to eat. They're quick to tell you their favorites.

Jared Randall says, "Beets, beans, and carrots are my very favorites. I love pumpkins and rhubarb. I like peas and corn. I don't really like tomatoes, but I do eat them. I DON'T LIKE ASPARAGUS AND EGGPLANT."

Children who eat homegrown produce value its taste. My son David, who teases me that his recollection of gardening was that it was a lot of work, admits, "The eating—that was wonderful, all except the zucchini. We grew far too much of that. Peas were the best, and raspberries, and fresh lettuce, and asparagus."

Jamie's mother says, "Two years ago we ran out of peas from the garden and bought them frozen. Nobody

would eat them. The tastes are definitely different!"

Children raised on fresh-picked may be surprised by a first encounter with tasteless veggies. My older son Chips says, "I liked the idea that we were growing vegetables, but I didn't realize how good they were until I went to college." His fervent request for a special meal on his first visit home? "Three fresh vegetables on my plate would be better than filet mignon, Mom!"

Choose for success
If a child is planning his own garden, help him to order seeds for quick-to-germinate, easy-to-grow vegetables. Look for disease-resistant varieties. Radishes, beans, and squash (including pumpkins) are especially good for a beginner. Leaf lettuce, dwarf peas, and beets need a little more skill. A

compact tomato plant won't require a lot in the way of staking. Most children love carrots, but may need some assistance in sowing them and keeping them moist, because the seeds are tiny and may not germinate for two weeks. For a novel twist, try planting a seed tape for carrots (see p. 56).

Choose for fun
Include some "fun" crops, fascinating to children for their surprises.

■ *Purple-podded bush beans* are easy to find among the leaves at harvest time. When placed in boiling water, they turn green in three minutes, the time recommended for blanching before freezing. They taste the same as conventional snap beans.

■ *Triple Treat pumpkins* produce seeds without hulls. Roast them for delicious and healthful snacks. Cook and eat the pumpkin flesh, or carve them into Jack-O-Lanterns.

■ *Spaghetti squash* looks like an oval yellow melon when ripe. Boil or bake, then open it for a surprise. Scoop out the flesh, and fluff it up with a fork. It looks like spaghetti. Serve it hot with sauce or cold in salads.

■ *Gourds* can't be eaten, but they grow in a myriad of shapes and colors. Dry them for bird houses, musical instruments, and decorations.

■ *Dwarfs* produce crops on miniature plants. Try Pixie or Tiny Tim tomatoes, midget corn, and Tom Thumb lettuce.

■ *Sunflowers* are exciting because they're giants.

■ *Snap peas* are wonderful for nibbling right from the garden. Eat pod and all—no shelling required.

■ *Peanuts* are unique in the way they set their pods. Each bright yellow flower sends a stalk down into the soil. Underground, these "pegs" produce clusters of peanuts at their tips. Peanuts grow best in the south, as they need four or five months of hot weather.

GET A HEAD START IN WINTER

Make plant markers
Have you a budding Cezanne in the family? A child's drawings of vegetables, done from life on a lazy summer day, or in winter from supermarket purchases, can be copied on pieces of wood or Masonite, painted with oil-base or acrylic paints, affixed to stakes, and used to mark garden beds next spring. If that sounds too ambitious, let her help you letter plain markers in anticipation of the spring rush. Use a permanent felt-tipped marking pen or a grease pencil.

Build and repair
While cold winds blow outdoors, a child can help you prepare A-frames for cucumbers or support devices for tomatoes or peas, or refurbish and sharpen tools (see Chapter 4).

Start seeds indoors
If you have space and the interest, help your child start vegetable, flower, or herb seedlings indoors. Buy pre-planted kits from seed houses, or prepare your own flats. This can be an exciting activity if you have a good light source, but discouraging, producing spindly, weak seedlings, if you do not (see project "Start Your Own Seedlings," p. 48).

SPRING, AT LAST!

Give soil the squeeze-a-handful test (see p. 35) to see if it's ready to dig. Teach the child that there are cool-weather crops and warm-weather crops. With the exception of peas, most of the cool-weather crops are those in which we eat leaves (spinach, lettuce, cabbage), stalks (celery, rhubarb), or roots (radishes, carrots, beets). Most fruits (cucumbers, tomatoes, peppers, eggplant, squashes, beans) are tender and should not go into the garden until the soil is warm and danger of frost is past.

Helping in the family garden
Most children love to plant. Let them participate in a way that suits their age, your planting system, and your temperament. Children want to feel important and a part of things, even if their role is as simple as pushing soil over seeds.

"This is the most exciting thing I've done in the garden," Paddy McCarthy reported to his classmates the first Monday in June. "I got to cover up the corn seeds my dad planted AND my dad planted my corn plant from school!"

Carol Newell says, "Potatoes are the most fun for kids. They love to drop the pieces in . . . and digging them up is like finding buried treasure!"

Black plastic magic
In the Coleman family garden, Tom lays large sheets of 3-mil black plastic on the garden, maps out planting distances, and zaps the plastic with a propane torch wherever he wants a planting hole. The pre-spaced holes make it easy for kids to help.

This year, seven-year-old Jamie and five-year-old Christie planted all the corn while Dad planted carrots and beans. Next season, the same plastic will be used for corn in a different place in the garden, to achieve crop rotation.

Black plastic retains heat and moisture and smothers weeds. Crops grow faster and produce faster. Jamie illustrates that by standing next to one of "his" corn plants on Independence Day weekend. "Knee high by the Fourth of July, but it's up to my head!" he announces proudly.

▲ **Andy and Peter help their dad dig potatoes.**

◀ **Make plant markers in winter.**

A-FRAME

▲ **Building an A-frame for cukes or other climbers is a good winter project.**

AWAY FROM IT ALL

▶ **A hideout provides a cozy retreat for Trevor.**

A plot of their own
If you decide to give a child a plot of his own, you may want to start him off with an easy-to-plant, little-to-weed kit (see Resources, p. 203). You may opt instead to give a child her own plot to plan from scratch. Remember to balance the child's need for independence with her yearning for encouragement and occasional guidance.

Messing around
Judy Adams has found giving her two daughters a space of their own is definitely worthwhile. Before she did this she was always saying, "No, no, that's planted too close together. No, no, no, don't pull that; it's not a weed." Now she gives each of her girls a patch of garden, seeds, and plant divisions and lets them go.

"The four-year-old just lets things happen. The eight-year-old may come to me if something didn't work and ask why, and then I can say, 'Well, maybe you could try this.'"

Judy is willing to give her children a place to "mess around," and time to explore and experiment without constant direction from an adult or continuing expectation for products or perfection. The girls may not have in-

stant success, but they're learning a lot about how things grow, and wondering why when they don't.

Raised beds
A child's garden often mirrors parents' methods. In graphic artist Rob Randall's vegetable garden, raised beds surround a central asparagus patch, making a pleasing tapestry of shape and texture. Paths between the beds are mulched impeccably with hay.

Next to their parents' garden, Jared and Caleb have smaller versions. Each has a two-and-a-half-foot-wide raised bed, framed by a hay-mulched path. Jared points to the crops in his garden. "I planted beets, carrots, and corn. Here's the corn plant I started in school. This is a cherry tomato in a wire cage, wax beans, green beans, and snow peas. My mother helped me with my garden, mostly by weeding it, but now I do a lot of it."

Whimsy
A bit of whimsy makes the garden fun. Tim Link named cucumber and squash hills for mountains. He made fancy signs, which his mom laminated and attached to popsicle sticks. He had Mount Everest, Mount McKinley, Mount Mansfield, Mount Greylock, and Mount Anthony—all in his garden.

GARDEN CARE: OF WEEDS AND BUGS

Don't expect too much in the way of weeding once initial gardening enthusiasm fades. Organic mulch or black plastic will help reduce this chore. Otherwise, be prepared either to lend a hand if asked (certainly you can help distinguish weeds from crop seedlings), or to turn the other way.

Companion planting helps to discourage bugs. Marigolds, nasturtiums, onions, and herbs among the vegetables lend a gay touch to a child's garden or your own.

Many children enjoy hand-picking

harmful insects, such as Japanese beetles. Megan, Sean, and Katie Lambert help their dad in this way. "We pick bugs off plants and drown them in water. Then we dump them on the compost pile," explains Sean.

THE HARVEST

Here's where children can be a big help. Many hands make less work shelling peas, snapping green beans, or husking corn. Old-time husking bees still have their parallels in the family garden.

In my family, camaraderie accompanied the bean harvest. The "Bennington Rural Volunteer Bean Cutters" assembled after each picking. We four sat around a mountain of snap beans, green in the white circle of the kitchen table, singing and joking as we removed stems and cut beans in preparation for blanching and freezing a winter's supply, each of us trying to devise a more efficient system than the others.

In some families, children are given the responsibility for picking, leaving adults free to cut and process. For big projects, they set up an assembly line.

When corn is ready, everyone in the Coleman family pitches in. The children help their dad pick and shuck while their mom begins blanching. When the shucking is done, the children help with the processing. Jamie bags the corn. Christie puts on the ties. In one afternoon, they get a year's worth into the freezer.

Remember to tailor your harvesting expectations to the age of the child. Very young children need a lot of guidance (see Chapter 2). Don't expect a five-year-old to pick five gallons of peas. Give a small child a small container and let him feel a part of an important family activity.

HIDEOUT

Sometimes, a child needs an escape from the garden—a place to retreat to when his interest is exhausted, but Mom or Dad is still intent on weeding the onions instead of having a tea party, tossing a softball, or going for a swim.

Eight-year-old Sean Lambert rearranged his dad's wood pile into a hideout. He often plays in it when Dad works in the garden. "It can be a place to hide away in or to get away from the noise," he says. "I go back there and play with my figures of men, or I pretend I'm on a ship in the ocean."

In a nearby hideout, whether it be like Sean's, a tree house, a tent, or a bean pole tepee (see p. 72), a child can feel a part of the tilling of earth even though she's not at the moment an active participant. The scraping sound of the hoe, spade, or rake, the smell of the earth, the warmth of the sun, the brush of the breeze, and the coziness of the hideout combine to create a pleasant atmosphere the child will always associate with gardens and growing.

START YOUR OWN SEEDLINGS

Get a jump on spring, when everyone is tired of winter.

What about light?
Light is essential! A greenhouse or window greenhouse is ideal, but few people have that luxury. A sunny southern window with a wide sill is fine. Otherwise, you'll need artificial light to ensure success.

You can pay a fortune for a fancy plant stand, or you can be resourceful and rig up your own system. Buy a four-foot-long, two-tube fluorescent fixture in a hardware or discount department store. Fit it with one "cool-white" bulb and one "daylight" bulb (or one horticultural light if you are raising flowers. Horticultural lights have the full spectrum of light contained in sunlight.). Hook up a timer to turn lights on and off. Set it for 14 to 18 hours of light a day.

A place to grow
Hang the fluorescent fixture over an old table, above a shelf, or above a 2-foot by 4-foot piece of plywood supported by a couple of sawhorses. Use hooks and adjustable chains to keep the light fixture four to six inches from seedlings.

Put the seed-starting rig wherever you have extra space, as long as the temperature is from 68 to 77°F in the day and up to 10°F colder at night. (If your house is too cool, find a spot near the water heater or furnace.) One of my friends uses part of her basement. She has painted the walls white to increase

light reflection even more.

Grow without soil
Buy a commercial, soil-less mix (a sterile blend of sphagnum peat moss, perlite, and vermiculite) designed especially for seed starting. Then you won't have to worry about damping-off, that mysterious fungus that makes seemingly healthy seedlings suddenly keel over dead. The mix has no weed seeds, the right amount of fertilizer to keep seedlings happy for four weeks or more, and is fluffy and spongy so there are plenty of air spaces for rapid root growth.

When you buy the mix, it will be very dry. Before you put it in planting containers, add water and mix thoroughly to moisten.

Containers galore
Use half-gallon cardboard milk cartons laid sideways, with the top side removed and the open end securely taped closed. Or keep them upright for tomato or pumpkin seedlings and you won't have to repot. Punch drainage holes in the bottom.

Use plastic or fiberboard seed trays, clear plastic shoeboxes with covers (put an inch of pebbles in the bottom for drainage), or plastic flower pots. Styrofoam cups, cottage cheese or yogurt containers, or foil loaf pans are fine, as long as you punch a few drainage holes in the bottom. Peat pots dry out really fast in winter's low-humidity houses, and are not recommended.

YOU NEED

- A good light source
- A place to set the seedlings
- Soil-less seed starting mix
- Planting containers
- Trays for the planting containers
- Seeds
- Chicken wire
- Water, watering can, spray-misting bottle
- Plastic wrap or plastic bags
- Timer (for artificial lights)
- Scissors

TIME OF YEAR

Four to six weeks before it's safe to set the plants in the garden. HOLD ON! It's better to start seeds a little too late than too early.

INSIDE

◀ **Jenny starts seeds under lights.**

▼ **Two 4-foot-long fluores-cent fixtures provide light for starting seedlings on this homemade plant stand.**

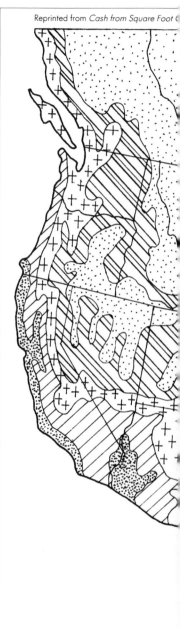

Whatever you choose, it should be at least three inches deep, and SCRUPU-LOUSLY *CLEAN.*

Put individual planting containers in large plastic trays or shallow pans, to catch the water that drains out.

What to plant?
Plant whatever needs a head start:

■ *Vegetables,* such as toma-toes, peppers, head lettuce, melons, winter squash, or broccoli

■ *Flowers,* such as marigolds and zinnias

■ *Herbs,* such as basil or par-sley. (These have *tiny* seeds and long germination peri-ods, and are recommended for older children with lots of patience. Soak parsley seeds in warm water for 24 hours before planting.)

A SAMPLING OF GERMINATION TIMES FOR VEGETABLE SEEDS

(These can be affected by soil temperature and moisture.)

4 TO 6 DAYS:
garden cress, radish

7 TO 10 DAYS:
bean, beet, cabbage fam-ily, corn, cucumber, lettuce, pea, spinach, squash family, tomato

10 TO 15 DAYS:
carrot, eggplant, pepper

12 TO 20 DAYS:
celery, parsnip

18 TO 24 DAYS:
parsley

When you grow your own transplants, you can choose exactly the variety you want.

How to plant
Put moist planting mix in the container. If the container does not have drainage holes, put a layer of pebbles or broken clay flower pot shards at the bottom before adding the planting mix. Sprinkle seeds on the mix, spacing at least an inch apart. (Lay a piece of chicken wire over the con-tainer and drop a seed through each hole.) Or plant two or three tomato, pepper, or squash seeds in one up-right half-gallon milk carton. Thin to one per container la-ter. Do the same in Styro-foam cups with flower or herb seeds.

Cover with mix twice as deep as the diameter of the seeds. Mist the planting mix to thoroughly dampen the seeds. Label the container with date and variety.

Make a greenhouse
Cover with plastic wrap or slip the container into a plas-tic bag and secure with a twist tie. If you use a plastic shoebox, merely put on the cover. When seedlings emerge, remove the cover-ing. Water whenever the surface is dry. After four weeks, feed with half-strength liquid fertilizer.

Snip, snip, snip
Thin the plants the easy way when they have their second set of leaves. With scissors, snip off weaker ones at

el Bartholomew (Garden Way Publishing 1985).

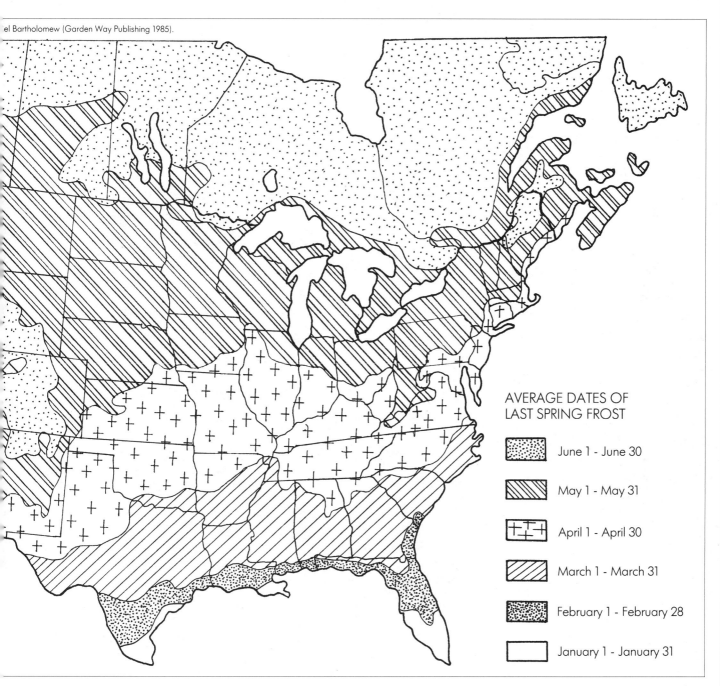

AVERAGE DATES OF
LAST SPRING FROST

June 1 - June 30

May 1 - May 31

April 1 - April 30

March 1 - March 31

February 1 - February 28

January 1 - January 31

ground level. Then you won't disturb fragile roots.

Harden off
Indoor seedlings are delicate. They must be introduced gradually to the outdoors. A week or two before setting them in the garden, begin putting them in a protected place outside, for short periods of time at

first, gradually increasing to a full day, and, finally, give them an overnight campout.

Get seedlings in plant trays ready to be separated from their friends. A week before transplanting, separate the plants by slicing a square around each with a knife. Do it again just before planting (see also Chapter 11, "Plant Experiments").

WHY DO WE START SEEDS INSIDE?

We start seeds inside to give plants a head start in climates where the outdoor growing season is too short for them to ripen or flower before killing frost in fall.

FOUR SQUARES FOR YOUNG GARDENERS

The fun of these gardens is that once plants are established they need little weeding. As they grow, the crops shade the soil completely, leaving no space for weeds. The few that appear can be pulled easily, or even ignored. Watering chores are reduced as well, and this makes a perfect kind of child's garden.

How big?
A 4-foot by 4-foot square is a good size for a child seven or older. If the child is younger, reduce the size to 3 by 3 so that shorter arms can reach the center of the garden without stepping in it.

Where?
Set a child's square in a corner of your vegetable garden or next to it. Lay a foot-wide path around the perimeter and mulch it heavily with straw, hay, or shredded bark, so the young gardener can walk around the patch without compacting cultivated soil. If you like, build up the soil in the square to make a raised bed. To make it really special, frame it with pressure-treated landscaping boards, available from most lumber yards.

Soil
Before planting, enrich the soil by mixing in compost, composted manure, or other organic matter, supplemented with bone meal and wood ashes, or a commercial vegetable fertilizer applied according to manufacturer's directions.

WHY DO PLANTS GROW UP?

Plants grow toward light—the sun outdoors or artificial light indoors.

Quick 'n' easy
The easiest of the four gardens is the mixed salad bed. Companion planting is used in the marigold and bean garden. Peas and carrots are a cool-weather variation. All these produce a crop in two months or less.

A step up
The Patchwork Salad Quilt is the most challenging of the four gardens, and is suggested for older children with some adult guidance and encouragement.

GROW A MIXED SALAD BED

An all-in-one garden

Feed the soil
Spread a 2- to 4-inch layer of compost or composted manure on the square, sprinkle with fertilizer, dig it in, hoe the clods, and rake smooth.

Toss the salad before planting!
Mix some of each kind of seed together in the pail, and sprinkle the mixture thinly

HARVESTING

▲ **Katie harvests lettuce for a supper salad.**

PREPARATION

◄ **Sean, Katie, and Megan Lambert get the soil ready for a mixed salad bed.**

and evenly over the square.

Put a blanket on the seeds
Sprinkle sifted compost or fine soil over the seeds to a depth of ¼ inch (½ inch in sandy soil). With the back of a hoe or the palm of your hand, firmly tamp down the soil to make good contact with the seeds.

Give the seeds a drink
Water with a gentle, fine spray from a watering can or hose. Don't let the bed dry out before seedlings germinate. Check it daily.

What will happen?
In less than a week, the radish seedlings should sprout. In about ten days, you'll have spinach and lettuce seedlings. See if you can tell them apart.

Rake-thin the seedlings
When the seedlings are 1 inch high, stand on one side and place the rake on the opposite edge of the square. Push the tines about one inch into the soil and pull the rake across the bed toward you. After you've done

the width of the bed in this direction, move to the side perpendicular to the place you started, and repeat the process, making a cross-hatch pattern with the rake. You will drag out some of the excess seedlings. It seems cruel, but if you leave them planted too thickly, they won't have enough room to grow.

Pick a bowl of salad
In three to four weeks, the radishes will be ready to eat. When you pull them, pull spinach and lettuce thinnings, too. Wash, spin or pat dry, toss with dressing, and feast on a fresh spring salad!

After the radishes have been pulled, either keep thinning the greens or cut off their tops with a scissors, and they will sprout again.

PLANT MARIGOLDS AND BUSH BEANS, NATURE'S PARTNERS

Marigolds help repel the Mexican bean beetle, and their gay border makes this garden as pretty as it is practical.

Feed the soil
Spread compost and a sprinkling of bone meal or fertilizer on the bed, dig it in, hoe the clods, and rake smooth. Set a stone or piece of slate in the center of the square, to serve as a stepping stone (optional).

INOCULATING

▲ **Jared pours powdered inoculant into the jar of moistened bean seeds. Then he will cover the jar and shake it to coat each seed with the black powder.**

Plant a frame of flowers
If the marigold seedlings are in a flat, cut the roots between the plants with a knife a few days before planting, and again on planting day. Then each plant with its roots will be easier to separate from the others.

With a trowel, make holes about a foot apart and 4 inches in from the edge of the square (see plan). Place each seedling in a hole so that it is as deep as it was in the flat. Fill in the soil and firm it around each plant.

Inoculate the bean seeds
You don't need a syringe and

needle for this inoculation, just a small jar with a cover. Legume inoculant, which looks like black powder, adds a fresh culture of nitrogen-fixing bacteria to the seed, so you'll have a bigger and better crop of beans. Put the seeds in the jar, moisten with a bit of water, pour out the excess, and add enough inoculant to coat the beans when you shake the jar.

Plant the beans
With a stick, trace a 30-inch by 30-inch square inside the marigold frame. With your finger, poke inch-deep holes about 4 inches apart around

the edge of this square and in rows across the center, making an overall pattern.

Drop an inoculated seed into each hole. Try to keep as much of the black powder as you can on the seed. Cover with soil, and tamp firmly with the back of a hoe or the palm of your hand.

Water the square
Water the bean area with a fine spray. Settle the soil around the roots of each marigold seedling with a fine trickle of water. To help the marigolds get a quick start, use a half-strength solution of fish emulsion or liquid fertilizer.

Care for the square
Cultivate around the marigold seedlings with a weeding hoe or small claw. Snip off dead blooms, and the plants will make more flowers. The beans should sprout in a week or ten days. Soon they will shade the soil so few weeds will grow.

Pick beans for supper
Watch the tiny beans form from the bean flowers. When they are big enough to eat, but still slim, carefully hold the plant with one hand and pull the beans with the other. They will be tender and delicious if you pick them before they get bumpy.

What next?
The harvest should last for about two weeks. When it is over, dig up a bean plant to discover the magic factories on its roots. Look for little round "nodules." Under a magnifying glass, they look

YOU NEED

- A 4-foot by 4-foot square of garden (3 by 3 for little tykes)
- Compost and bone meal, or garden fertilizer (Neither beans nor marigolds are heavy feeders.)
- Spade, hoe, garden rake, trowel, ruler, and paring knife
- Flat stone or piece of slate (optional)
- 12 marigold seedlings (Make sure they're hardened off.)
- Bush bean seeds
- Legume inoculant
- A small jar with cover
- A watering can or hose with fine spray nozzle

WHEN TO PLANT

When danger of frost is past and the ground has warmed up

TIME TO HARVEST

Eight weeks

TAMPING

▲ **Caleb and Jared firm the soil after dropping inoculated bush bean seeds into holes spaced 4 inches apart. They're careful not to step in the square.**

◀ **(BOTTOM) Planting plan, Marigolds and Bush Beans**

12 marigolds

Beans

stone

30"

9"   9"

like miniature potatoes. That is where a special bacteria lives. It takes nitrogen from the air and makes it available to plants.

Thank the soil
The best thing you can do for your soil now is to turn under the bean plants right there where they are growing. You may need help from a grownup. Then just sit back and enjoy the marigolds for the rest of the summer. If you want to have a fall garden, plant some lettuce or spinach in the center of the square.

PLANT PEAS AND CARROTS, COOL-WEATHER FRIENDS

We suggest a seed tape for the carrots, because planting carrot seeds thinly is a tedious job.

Feed the soil
Spread a couple of inches of compost, some garden fertilizer (optional), and a sprinkling of wood ashes on the soil, dig it in, hoe the clods, and rake smooth. Both peas and carrots like the extra potash the wood ashes provide.

Inoculate the peas
See p. 54.

Plant peas the easy way
Mark out a 30-inch by 30-inch square in the center of the plot. Sprinkle the pea seeds evenly over the surface

CARROTS

▲ **Bear and Bree lay the seed tape for carrots in the furrow.**

of this inner square. Try to get the seeds 2 or 3 inches apart. Then rake the seeds into the soil, so that they are 1 to 2 inches deep. Tamp down with the back of a hoe or the palm of your hand.

Plant a tape of carrots
Carrot seeds are so tiny that planting a seed tape instead saves a lot of work. Use a hoe to make a furrow about 4 inches from the outer edge

of the square. Lay the tape in the furrow and cover it with ½ inch of fine soil. The paper tape will soon dissolve.

Water the bed
Soak the square with a fine spray. Keep everything moist until the seeds sprout.

What next?
Peas should be up in six to ten days. Carrots will take from ten days to two weeks. After the seedlings are up,

WHAT DO ROOTS DO?

Roots reach into the soil and bring up minerals and water to help a plant grow. Roots also anchor a plant in the ground.

cultivate around the carrots to keep down weeds. To save work, lay down some mulch. The pea vines will intertwine and hold each other up. There won't be much room for weeds between them. Watch pea pods form from the flowers.

Pick peas
Shell peas or snap peas are ready to pick when they are fat with peas. Pick snow peas while the pods are still flat. Hold the vine with one hand and tug the pod with the other. The best thing about peas is to be able to pop some into your mouth and taste the crunchy sweetness right there in the garden.

Continue with carrots
Harvest baby carrots at the same time as peas. If the soil is really fluffy, you may be able to pull out a carrot by grasping the stem near the ground. If the stem breaks off when you try this, dig up the carrots with a trowel. Leave the rest of the carrots to grow larger, and harvest some any time you want a crunchy snack.

Thank the soil
Peas, like beans, are legumes, with bumps on the roots called nodules that are the homes of nitrogen-fixing bacteria. When the pea harvest is over, give nutrients back to the soil by digging in the pea vines right in place.

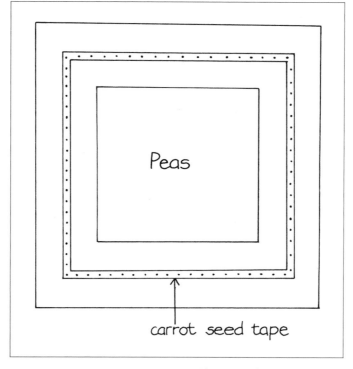

carrot seed tape

PEAS AND CARROTS SALAD FACES
YOU NEED:

2 medium-sized carrots

½ cup sugar snap peas, shelled

2 sugar snap peas in the pod

1 lemon slice

Grate carrots. Divide grated carrots between two plates. Decorate with green peas—making hair, eyes and a nose with individual peas and a mouth with the whole pea. Squeeze lemon over all. Serves 2.

▲ **Planting plan, Peas and Carrots**

HARVESTING

▶ **Ny, Vy, and Ben harvest peppers.**

CREATE A PATCHWORK SALAD QUILT

Kitchen herbs make good companions for salad vegetables—basil, chives, and parsley with tomatoes; basil with lettuce; and chives with carrots.

Feed the soil
Spread a thick (4 inches or more) layer of compost or composted manure, and a sprinkling of bone meal and wood ashes on the soil, dig it in, hoe, and rake smooth.

Lay out the patchwork
With sticks and string, mark off a 1-foot-wide "frame" around the edge of the square. Mark off 1-foot intervals along the outer edge of the large square, and, with your finger, divide the frame into twelve 1-foot squares.

Plant the quilt
The planting plan shows the contents of each square.
■ GREENS. Mix the lettuce and spinach seeds, broadcast them in the large center square, cover with fine soil, tamp down, and treat as a mixed salad bed (p. 52).
■ CHIVES. Set a clump of chives in each of the two corners on the southern edge of the square. Plant at the same level they were growing.
■ PARSLEY. In one square between the chives, set four parsley seedlings. Save the other square for the sweet basil.
■ CARROTS. Plant a square of carrots on each side, just

YOU NEED

- A 4-foot by 4-foot square of garden
- Compost or composted manure, bone meal and wood ashes, or garden fertilizer
- Spade, hoe, garden rake, and trowel
- A ruler, string, and sticks
- Carrot, radish, spinach, and assorted leaf lettuce seeds
- 16 onion sets
- 2 small clumps of chives
- Seedlings (hardened off):
  4 parsley
  6 to 9 sweet basil
  2 sweet pepper
  2 compact tomato (i.e., Pixie or Tiny Tim)
- A few matches (optional)
- 2 small wire tomato cages
- A watering can or hose with fine spray nozzle
- Mulch (straw, hay, grass clippings, or 1-foot by 4-foot black plastic)

WHEN TO PLANT

Early spring for everything but the basil, tomatoes, and peppers. Wait until frost danger is past before setting them in the garden.

TIME TO HARVEST

Three weeks to three months

◀ **Aaron picks a ripe tomato.**

▼ **Planting plan, Patchwork Salad Quilt. (For an even simpler, 2- by 4-foot garden, plant just the front and back rows!)**

above the chives. Poke sixteen holes in the square and place two or three seeds in each hole. Cover with ¼ inch of fine soil, and tamp down.

■ RADISHES. Above the carrots on one side, plant radishes in the same way as carrots, but cover the seeds with ½ inch of soil.

When the carrots and radishes sprout, snip off all but one seedling in each of the sixteen spots in the square.

■ ONIONS. Poke sixteen holes in the onion square and put an onion set in each hole. Barely cover with fine soil.

Water the square
Soak the soil thoroughly with a fine spray. Keep moist until seedlings sprout.

Add warm-weather crops
■ SWEET BASIL. Set the seedlings in the reserved square. Firm the earth around them. According to folklore, basil keeps away witches!

■ SWEET PEPPERS. Set a pepper plant in each of the last two corners. Bury a few match heads under them (but not touching the roots) to supply extra sulfur. Put a little extra compost and bone meal under the roots, too.

■ TOMATOES. Pinch off the lower leaves of the tomato. Dig a planting hole in the center of each of the last two squares, deep enough to cover the stem where you have removed the leaves.

N
↑

1 pepper	1 cherry tomato	1 cherry tomato	1 pepper
16 onions	Mixed lettuces and spinach		16 radishes
16 carrots			16 carrots
1 chives	4 parsley	9 basil	1 chives

(New roots will sprout along the buried stem, making a stronger plant.) Mix compost and bone meal in the planting hole. Set each tomato plant, fill in the soil, and press it firmly into the earth. Set a small wire tomato cage over each plant.

Settle the seedlings
Water each seedling with a fine trickle of half-strength fish emulsion or liquid fertilizer.

Insulate the soil
Put a 4- to 6-inch carpet of mulch on the soil around the peppers and tomatoes. If you use black plastic, lay it down BEFORE you plant, make

holes for the seedlings, and plant through the holes.

A LONG HARVEST

Pull radishes when ready. Keep snipping parsley, basil, and chives for the cook to put in salads or other dishes. Cut the tops of lettuce and it will sprout again. Pull young onions to use as scallions and let some grow large. Carrots are delicious as babies or grownups. Cut peppers from the plant with an inch of stem. Ripe cherry tomatoes are fun to pop into your mouth still warm from the sun, while you're picking some for tonight's salad.

GROW PERSONALIZED PUMPKINS

Harvest a pumpkin inscribed with your initials. Make some for your best friends, too.

YOU NEED

- An 8-foot by 8-foot square of rich soil
- A bushel of compost and/or manure
- Lime and bone meal, or garden fertilizer
- A spade, hoe, and rake
- An 8-foot by 8-foot square of black plastic, or organic mulch such as straw or hay
- Pumpkin seeds
- A watering can or hose
- Manure tea (see p. 36), liquid fertilizer, or fish emulsion
- A pencil and paring knife

WHEN TO PLANT

When danger of frost is past and the ground has warmed up

TIME TO HARVEST

Four months

Soak the seeds
The night before you plant your pumpkins, put the seeds in lukewarm water to soak.

Feed the soil
Pumpkins are sprawling, heavy feeders, so give them plenty of room and plenty of fuel. Some people plant pumpkin seeds right in the compost pile, where their food supply is unlimited. Usually, pumpkins are planted in a "hill," with treasure buried underneath, only in this case, the "treasure" is manure 'n' stuff, instead of gold.

Dump a bushelful of well-rotted manure and/or compost in the center of the 8-foot by 8-foot plot. Add a handful of lime and a bit of bone meal, or some garden fertilizer. Shovel soil on top of the rich pumpkin food to form a hill.

Blanket the soil
If you decide to use black plastic to help give your pumpkins heat and save you the job of weeding, spread it on the ground before you plant the seeds. Anchor the edges with soil or rocks. Cut a hole in the plastic at the top of the pumpkin hill.

If you use hay, straw, or the like, spread a 6-inch to 1-foot thick layer on the square after planting.

Plant the seeds
Poke six to eight holes in the soil about an inch deep, place a pumpkin seed in each, and cover with soil.

AN EARLY START

If you live in the North, you can give your pumpkins a head start on a short growing season by starting them indoors six weeks before it's safe to put them outdoors.

Soak seeds in lukewarm water overnight. Fill half-gallon milk cartons with planting mix. Plant two seeds 1 inch deep in each carton. Cover with plastic wrap and set in a sunny, warm place or under grow lights. After the seedlings sprout, remove wrap and snip off the weaker plant with a scissors.

Give a boost of liquid fertilizer every two weeks. Harden off for a week before transplanting to the garden.

Prepare the hills and dig holes for the seedlings. Cut off the bottom of the milk carton, set it in the planting hole, and carefully slip the carton up and off. Pumpkin seedlings do not like to have their roots disturbed!

SHOWING OFF

▶ **Jamie and Chris are delighted with their personalized pumpkins!**

Tamp down with the palm of your hand.

Give the seeds a drink
This will be the first of many, as pumpkins are thirsty growers and need lots of water. Soak the hill with a gentle spray of water.

Survival of the fittest
The seeds should sprout in seven to ten days. After the seedlings are up and sturdy, snip off all but two or three of the most vigorous. It's hard to do, but you don't want too much competition for the food under the hill.

Keep weedin' and feedin'
The mulch should smother most weeds. Pull out the few that may sprout between the seedlings.

Every two weeks, give your vines a booster feeding of manure tea (see p. 36), fish emulsion, or other liquid fertilizer.

Watch them grow
Your vines will grow and grow. Watch for flowers. The ones on long stems are males. Tiny pumpkins will form at the base of female flowers.

Personalize a pumpkin
When you find a young pumpkin that's off to a good start, trace your initials on the surface with a pencil. With a paring knife, go over the initials, adding enough

light pressure to break the skin of the pumpkin. Then watch your initials grow as the pumpkin grows! If you pick off small flowers that form near the ends of the vines, the pumpkins nearest the hill may grow larger.

How to harvest
Pumpkins are ready when the rind is orange and hard. Harvest before hard frost by cutting from the vine. Make sure you leave a 3- to 4-inch stem on the pumpkin, or it will not keep.

WHAT'S THE BEST SOIL LIKE?

The best soil is moist and fluffy. Do you know how to make it that way? Add lots and lots of organic matter.

WATERING

▲ Chris gives his pumpkin seeds a good start with a thorough soaking.

INSCRIBING

▶ The pumpkin vines responded well to their buried treasure of compost and manure. Chris carves his name on a green pumpkin.

PUMPKIN FUN

After you harvest, try these activities:

■ Lift your pumpkins. Guess how much they weigh. Put them on a scale to find out.

■ Measure the circumferences. Does the fattest one weigh the most?

■ Guess how many seeds are in a pumpkin. Count the seeds into groups of tens. Sort into hundreds, tens, and ones. How close was your guess?

■ Cook the seeds for a tasty snack. Wash and pat dry. Mix 2 cups seeds with 2 teaspoons oil and a sprinkling of sea salt. Spread out on a cookie sheet. Roast in a 300°F oven until golden, about ½ to 1 hour, stirring every 10 or 15 minutes. Eat!

■ Make a pumpkin seed necklace. Rinse some of the seeds. Let dry overnight or longer. Use a needle and heavy thread to string them together.

■ Make a Jack-O-Lantern. Will it be happy, sad, or scary?

■ Cook pumpkin flesh, puree it, and eat as a vegetable or use it to make pumpkin pie. Ask a grownup to help you.

■ Read some pumpkin poems. Try "Peter, Peter, Pumpkin Eater" by Mother Goose, or "Theme in Yellow" by Carl Sandburg.

DID YOU KNOW…

The largest pumpkin yet recorded weighed in at more than 500 pounds?

PLANT CORN, NATIVE AMERICAN STYLE

Hills of corn, pole beans, and squash.

YOU NEED

- A 9-foot by 9-foot (or larger) square of garden
- Compost and/or well-rotted manure
- Bone meal, and wood ashes or lime
- A fish or fish entrails for each hill (optional)
- Spade, hoe, and rake
- Corn, pole bean, and squash seeds
- Legume inoculant
- A small jar with cover
- A watering can or hose
- Mulching material
- Manure tea, fish emulsion, or liquid fertilizer

WHEN TO PLANT

When danger of frost is past and the ground is warm. Native Americans planted corn when emerging oak leaves were the size of squirrels' ears.

TIME TO HARVEST

Two-and-a-half to three months (Three-and-a-half to four months for popcorn and flint corn)

Wear an Indian headband when you plant these "three sisters," and pretend you lived long ago. The companionship of interplanting helps these vegetable friends. Corn provides support for the pole beans and a windbreak and shade for the squash. Beans produce nitrogen for the corn. Squash keeps the corn roots cool and discourages marauding raccoons, who don't like to walk on their prickly leaves.

Feed the soil
Corn and squash have huge appetites. To satisfy them, prepare soil in fall. Dig in gobs of manure or plant a cover crop to turn under in spring (see Chapter 5, "Let's Dig!").

Lay out the hills
Space a minimum of nine hills 2½ to 3 feet apart in three or more rows, forming a "block." Corn must be planted in this way, rather than in one long row, so that, when the wind blows, the pollen from the male tassels of one plant can get to the female silks on the ears of another plant. Otherwise, the kernels will not develop at the base of the silks.

Bury some "treasure" of compost and/or manure, bone meal, and wood ashes or lime under each hill. Add a trash fish or entrails from the fish market. Form the hills as described for personalized pumpkins (p. 62).

Inoculate the bean seeds
See p. 54.

Plant the seeds
In each hill, poke holes and plant four or five seeds each of corn, beans, and squash. Cover with about an inch of soil.

Give the seeds a drink
Soak well with water after planting, and water regularly. Corn is an especially thirsty plant.

Blanket the soil
To save later weeding, spread a thick carpet of mulch over the planting area.

What next?
The seeds should sprout in seven to ten days. Snip off all but two or three strongest seedlings of each vegetable. When the corn is about 6 inches high, give the crops a drink of manure tea, fish emulsion, or liquid fertilizer. Do it again when the corn is knee high. Help the bean vines find the corn stalks, so they can climb up.

Harvesting hints
SWEET CORN ears are ripe when the silks are brown, the husks are dark green, and the juice from a punctured kernel is milky. If it is watery, it's not quite ready to pick, and if there's no juice, it's too late! Harvest in the afternoon, when sugar content is highest. In fact, have the water boiling in the pot before you pick it!

Leave POPCORN, FLINT CORN, and DENT CORN on the stalk until the kernels are hard and dry. Then carefully peel back the husks, and hang the corn on a wire or rope you've stretched out in a dry, well-ventilated place. When the kernels are dry, guess how many are on one ear. Strip them from the cob and count to find out.

For harvesting hints for POLE BEANS and SQUASH, see pp. 75 and 64.

WHAT SEED VARIETIES WILL YOU CHOOSE?

- CORN. Plant sweet corn, popcorn, Indian corn, or flint or dent corn (good for drying and grinding into meal). Plant only one variety in a garden space. If you mix species, they will cross-pollinate, and you may get sweet corn that's as tough as dent corn!
- POLE BEANS. See suggestions on p. 74.
- SQUASH. Grow one of the many kinds of winter squash, gourds, or pumpkins.

COMPANION PLANTING

▲ **Tadhg, Cordelia, and Rhea plant corn, pole bean, and squash seeds in each hill.**

A VEGETABLE WITH MANY USES

We eat corn in many ways: corn on the cob, corn fritters, corn pudding, corn flakes, corn bread, corn chips, tacos, enchiladas, corn oil margarine, cornstarch, corn syrup, and popcorn.

Early settlers used corncobs for checkers, toy animals, corncob pipes, and corncob jelly; and the husks for dolls and a medicinal tea.

WHY DO PEOPLE SAVE SEEDS?

People save seeds from plants that are NOT hybrids, to keep these varieties from becoming extinct (like the dinosaurs!). It may be a type of squash grandfather grew, or a flower variety we can no longer buy from a seed catalog, or a rare plant, or a kind of bean that is very resistant to disease or insects, or corn that is similar to the kind Native Americans grew. The Seed Savers Exchange in Decorah, Iowa, was organized to help gardeners everywhere exchange rare seeds.

PLANTING A HILL

▲ **Tadhg pokes each seed carefully into its place.**

CLOSEUP

◄ **Pole bean seeds will produce vines that climb the corn stalks.**

GRIND MEAL FOR CORN BREAD

Find a couple of large, flat stones, put on your Indian headband, and try to grind the hard kernels as these native Americans did. It's hard work!

Grind it the easy way, in a grain mill or coffee grinder.

Corn Bread
¾ cup cornmeal
¾ cup flour
2½ teaspoons baking powder
¾ teaspoon salt
1 egg
¾ cup milk
2½ tablespoons oil
1½ tablespoons honey

Mix dry ingredients. Beat remaining ingredients separately. Add the wet ingredients to the dry ingredients with a few quick strokes. Pour into a greased 8-inch by 8-inch pan. Bake at 425°F for 25 minutes. While the corn bread bakes, make butter.

Butter
Pour 1 cup heavy cream into a quart jar. Cover and shake. Let your friends share the shaking. Chant:

Come, butter, come.
Come, butter, come.
(name) 's at the garden gate
Waiting for a butter cake
Come, butter, come.

First you'll make whipped cream. Suddenly, the cream will separate into liquid buttermilk and solid butter. Pour off the buttermilk and push the butter together with a spatula to squeeze out all the liquid. Slather sweet butter on the warm corn bread when it comes out of the oven!

EXPLOSION

▲ **Catch and eat! Popcorn fireworks are exciting for children of all ages.**

DID YOU KNOW?

Corn has been around for a long, long time. The North American Indians grew it and introduced it to the Pilgrims in the 1600s. Columbus found it in the New World in 1492. Before that, the Incas grew it in Peru. In fact, corn fossils from 4000 B.C. have been discovered in Central America!

POPCORN FIREWORKS

YOU NEED

- Popcorn
- Oil
- Electric frypan
- Large, clean sheet

WHAT TO DO

Spread a clean sheet on the floor. Put an electric frypan in the center of the sheet. Add a bit of oil and pop the corn without covering the pan. Sit on the sheet and enjoy the explosion! Make sure you do this with a grownup.

▲ **Children in colonial times made corn husk dolls like these.**

MAKE A CORN HUSK DOLL

Prepare the husks
Soak the corn husks in warm water until they bend without cracking. Slit some into narrow strips to use for tying (or use yarn or string).

Form the body
■ HEAD: Lay several husks on top of each other. Fold in half. Tie under the fold to make a head.

■ ARMS: Slip some folded husks between the body husks, below the tie. Let them stick out on both sides to form arms. Tie at the place the "wrists" should be, and cut off the extra length of husk at the end of each "hand."

■ WAIST AND LEGS: Tie the body husks again under the arms, to make a waist. For a girl doll, arrange the lower part of the husks into a skirt. For a boy doll, separate the husks into two parts and tie at the "ankles."

Add hair and a face
Glue corn silk on the head for hair. Add features with colored markers.

Special touches
Use extra husks, corn silk, twigs, and buttons to make a broom, a rake, a pocketbook, a hat, or the like for your doll.

YOU NEED
■ Dried corn husks and corn silks
■ Water
■ Yarn or string
■ Scissors
■ Fine-point colored markers
■ White glue and brush

SHOW OFF!

Exhibit your prize vegetables in the County Fair. A harvest fair will often have a division especially for young gardeners.

How do you get ready for the fair?

Begin in spring
Nurture healthy crops, by enriching the soil before planting, weeding, watering, mulching, and picking off insect pests during the growing season. Occasionally, turn your pumpkins and squash to promote even ripening. Place a small board under each developing fruit to protect it from rot.

Get a schedule
Well ahead of the fair, ask your county agent for a list of the classes. This schedule will tell you what vegetables you can enter, and will give important information about how to prepare them for exhibit and what the judges will look for as they evaluate them.

Pick 'em fresh
To harvest the freshest vegetables, water thoroughly in early morning and pick just before you leave for the fair. Or pick the day of the fair and keep the produce in the refrigerator until you depart.

EXCEPTIONS are potatoes and onions. Pick them three to seven days before the fair, to allow time for drying. Dry potatoes away from sunlight to prevent greening.

Select the best
Choose well-ripened (but not over-mature), well-formed vegetables that are free from bruises, scars, or signs of insect damage. They should look delectable for eating! The largest specimens are not necessarily the winners (except in "giant" classes!). If an exhibit class requires you to show several specimens (i.e., five snap beans), pick a few more than you will need. Then choose those that are as much alike in size, shape, and color as possible. With a sponge or soft cloth, gently remove any clinging soil.

Pick to specifications
The schedule will give you exact requirements for exhibiting each vegetable. Here are some general guidelines:
- TOMATOES, PEPPERS, EGGPLANTS. Leave stem and calyx (the green, leaf-like sepals just above the fruit) attached.
- PUMPKINS, SQUASH. Leave 2 to 3 inches of stem attached.
- CARROTS, BEETS. Clean, but do not break the skin. Trim tops to 2 inches.
- CABBAGE, CAULIFLOWER. Leave outer leaves attached. Wash the head of cauliflower carefully.
- CORN. Leave on husks and silk. When you get to the fair, carefully slit a 1-inch-wide strip of husk and peel it back to expose two or three rows of kernels.
- ONIONS. Dry for a few days. Trim tops to 2 inches. Do not peel, but take off a couple of the outermost skins that are crusted with soil.
- SUNFLOWERS. Exhibit with 6 to 12 inches of stalk. Choose heads with no missing or damaged seeds.

Show off your giants
There's usually a class for heavyweight vegetables. Here's a chance to show that zucchini that grew too large to eat, or giant pumpkins or carrots.

Transport with care
Carefully wrap each vegetable in burlap, newspaper, or other covering. Pack carefully in a sturdy box to prevent bruising during the trip to the fair.

Information, please
When you get to the fair, you will be asked to fill out a tag for each entry. It's really important to include the name and VARIETY of each vegetable, so write it down before you leave home. Judges will deduct points if this information is not included.

Happy exhibiting!

FUN IN THE GARDEN

Three projects to prove that gardening is not all work and no play.

YOU NEED

- A 6-foot circle of garden
- Compost and bone meal or garden fertilizer
- A shovel, hoe, and rake
- Six to eight poles, 6 to 8 feet long
- Heavy twine or wire
- String and scissors
- Legume inoculant
- A small jar with cover
- Pole bean seeds
- A watering can
- Hay, straw, or black plastic
- One or two flat stones (optional)

WHEN TO PLANT

When danger of frost has passed and the ground has warmed up

TIME TO HARVEST

Two to three months

BUILD A POLE BEAN TEPEE

A living garden hideout that gives food as well as a shady retreat. Pretend you are Jack and watch your bean stalk climb toward the sky.

Feed the soil
Spread a couple of inches of compost and a sprinkling of bone meal or fertilizer on the bed and dig it in. Beans do not like a lot of manure, but they do like a bit of extra phosphorus (from the bone meal). Hoe the bed and rake it smooth.

Build a tepee skeleton
Set one end of each pole near the edge of the circular plot, spaced evenly around the circumference. Tie together the upper ends of the poles with wire or heavy twine, forming the frame of a tepee. It takes two people to handle all the pieces. Push the bottom end of each pole firmly into the earth.

Add climbing strings
Give your bean vines plenty of places to climb. Run a length of string down each pole and make x's of string between the poles. Tie them securely. Leave a space between the two poles that frame your "doorway."

Inoculate the bean seeds
Follow directions on page 54.

Plant the beans
Poke about six holes around the base of each pole, and

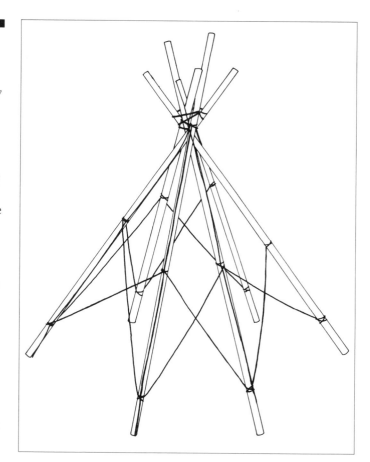

▲ **Pole bean tepee framework. Criss-crossed string gives bean vines many places to climb.**

FINISHED

▶ **Caleb and Jared harvest beans from inside the tepee.**

A PRIVATE PLACE

Invite a friend to share some lemonade inside your shady tepee, or hide there while grownups work in their own garden. Listen to the sounds outside. Make up a story about your special hideout, or, if you're really sleepy, spread out a blanket, grab a cuddly pillow, and snuggle in for a nap.

TEPEE TYING

▲ **Jared and Caleb discover that tying together the top of a pole bean tepee is a tricky job.**

HALFWAY

▶ **Bean vines begin to climb the tepee.**

POLE BEANS: WHAT VARIETY WILL YOU CHOOSE?

■ KENTUCKY WONDER are long, slim beans when young, with a delicious, nutty flavor. They can also be allowed to mature and used as shell beans.

■ ROMANO ITALIAN have flat, wide pods, and are very tender and delicate when picked young and often. They too can stay on the vine until the beans inside mature.

■ PURPLE PODDED have dark purple beans that turn green when cooked. They're easy to find among the green leaves!

■ SCARLET RUNNER is a giant. It grows to more than 10 feet tall, with huge leaves and large, bright red trumpet-shaped flowers. Hummingbirds may come to drink nectar from them. Cook and eat the beans inside the foot-long pods.

place an inoculated seed in each hole. Try to keep as much of the black powder as you can on the seeds. Cover seeds with an inch of soil, and tamp down with the palm of your hand or the back of a hoe.

Give the beans a drink
Sprinkle water on the planting area at the base of each pole until the ground is well soaked.

Avoid extra weeding
No sense weeding inside the tepee! Spread a thick layer of hay, straw, or other mulching material inside the poles and in the space around the outside, or cover the area with black plastic. Set one or two flat stones in the doorway of your tepee to serve as a threshold.

What next?
The beans should sprout in a week to ten days. Use a hoe to gently draw earth up against their stems. Pull out any small weeds that sprout between the seedlings.

Give young vines some extra food with a side dressing of 5-10-5 garden fertilizer or liquid plant food, such as fish emulsion. As they grow, guide the runners to nearby strings, so they will have a place to twine and climb. Watch the bean vines creep up your framework, until they form a shady hideout.

■ ONE CAUTION: Never touch bean plants when they are wet, or you may spread disease.

Harvest and hide
When the beans are ready for picking, hold the vine and gently pull off the pods. You will probably have to crawl inside the tepee to harvest many of the beans.

Keep picking the pods before the beans inside make them bumpy, and eat them like snap beans. Pole beans keep making new beans for a long time. If you get tired of picking them, let the pods stay on the vine until they are dry. Then use the beans inside as shell beans.

CUKE IN A BOTTLE

You've seen ships in bottles and wondered how they got there. Grow a cucumber in a bottle, and leave all your friends shaking their heads, wondering how you did it!

Capture the cuke
Slip a baby cucumber carefully into a narrow-necked bottle. Try to find a cucumber that is under many leaves, in good shade. Otherwise, make a "parasol" by laying a few sheets of newspaper or a piece of sheeting over the bottle, to protect it from the hot sun. Without shade, the tender cucumber will rot in the intense heat inside the bottle.

Watch it grow
As the cucumber grows, it will fill the bottle. Watch it carefully and cut the stem just before this happens. (The cuke may break the bottle if it continues to grow.) Ask your friends how they think you got it in there.

PICKLE THE PUZZLER

The fresh cucumber will last only a short time unless you preserve it. Boil 2 cups vinegar, 2 cups water, and 3 tablespoons pickling salt, pour the liquid over the cuke in the bottle, and put on the lid or cork. Now you have a pickle in a bottle. Let your friends wonder how you're going to get it out!

▼ **Gently push a developing cucumber through the neck of a bottle.**

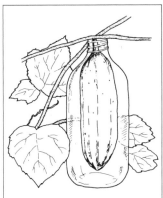

HARVEST TIME
▲ **Cut the cucumber from the vine when it has almost filled the bottle.**

YOU NEED
■ A cucumber vine with baby cukes forming

■ A narrow-necked bottle with a lid or cork

■ Newspaper or part of an old sheet

■ A knife

■ Vinegar, salt, and water for pickling (optional)

WHEN TO DO IT
When cucumbers are forming

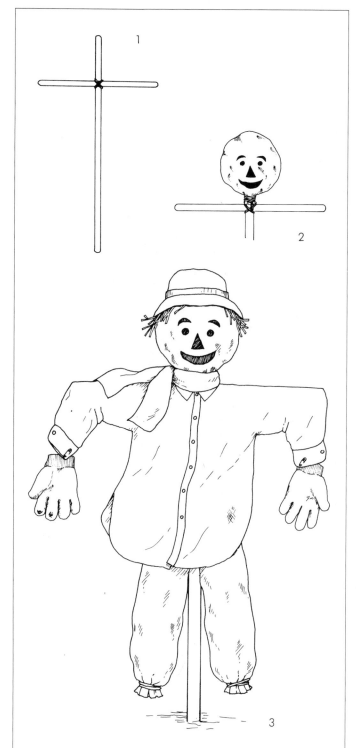

STEPS 1, 2, AND 3

▲ Tie the short pole per-
pendicular to the long pole.
Stuff and add a head.
Dress as you please!

DRAWING

▲ (TOP) Vy draws a face on
the sack with a permanent
marker.

TYING

▲ (BOTTOM) Vy, Ny, and
Ben work together to tie the
short pole firmly to the long
one.

ERECTING

▲(TOP) Up he goes! It's time to add a few finishing touches to our garden friend.

STUFFING

▲(BOTTOM) All hands help stuff the scarecrow with hay.

CREATE A SCARECROW

Make a funny friend in spring, to keep crows from eating your newly planted corn, or wait until fall, and use it for a seasonal decoration.

Build a skeleton
Make the "shoulders" by attaching the short pole perpendicular to the long one, about a foot from the top, and lashing the two together with heavy twine. Pound the long pole into the ground.

Make the head
Draw a silly face on the pillowcase, sack, or nylon stocking. Go over it with permanent markers, or stitch the features with yarn. Stuff the head with straw, hay, or dry leaves. Slide it over the top of the long pole and tie it around the "neck" with twine. Add a rag mop head or straw for hair, and pin on a hat.

Dress the scarecrow
Add and stuff a shirt, overalls or jeans, gloves, scarf, and whatever your scarecrow needs to be funny or scary. Give it a rake, hoe, broom, or pail. Have fun creating a personality to live in your garden!

YOU NEED

- Two poles, one 5 or 6 feet long, one 2 or 3 feet long
- Heavy twine
- A pillowcase, sack, or nylon stocking, permanent markers, yarn, or embroidery thread and needle
- A shirt
- Overalls or jeans
- A hat and hat pins
- Gloves
- Straw, hay, or dry leaves for stuffing
- Optional accessories: broom, rake, mop, scarf, etc.

TIME OF YEAR

Spring or fall

HAVE A NIBBLING PARTY IN THE GARDEN

Play Peter Rabbit, but get Mr. McGregor's permission first!

Pick some veggies

■ PEAS. Hold pea vines in one hand and pick pods with the other. Try sugar snap peas, shell peas, or snow peas.

■ CARROTS. Pull baby carrots from soft earth, or dig them up with a trowel.

■ LETTUCE. Pull thinnings, or cut off leaves with a scissors.

Wash them

Rinse the carrots and lettuce in the bucket of water. Drain them in the colander. Add unshelled snap or snow peas, and shelled garden peas.

Have a party!

Spread the bath towel or mat in a grassy, shady place. Set the colander of young veggies in the center. Sit down and help yourselves to tasty nibbles. Mmm, good!

OTHER GOOD NIBBLING VEGGIES

Baby snap beans, parsley, cherry tomatoes, radishes, garden cress, baby zucchini, scallions (IF you like onions!), baby new potatoes, and young spinach.

HEALTHY

▲ **(TOP) Rachaele, Allyson, and Felice get their vitamins straight from the garden.**

TASTY

▲ **(BOTTOM) Mmm, Sugar Snap peas taste scrumptious, too!**

YOU NEED

■ A large, clean towel or tatami mat
■ A bucket of clean water
■ A colander
■ Small paper plates (optional)
■ A garden with fresh peas, baby carrots, and lettuce
■ Permission to pick
■ Scissors and trowel

TIME OF YEAR

When peas are ready

TIME NEEDED

One hour or less

JUST PICKED

▶ **A quick rinse and this carrot will be ready for nibbling.**

BERRY PICKING FOR FAMILY FUN

Pick in your garden or visit a commercial farm on a pick-your-own day. Pick 'em and eat 'em: one for me, one for the bucket.

YOU NEED

- Ripe raspberries or highbush blueberries
- Small pails with handles (sandbox size is best)
- Rope
- Family or friends for companionship

TIME OF YEAR

Summer, when the berries are ripe

TIME NEEDED

An hour or less

A picking party
Gather your family or friends. Best time to pick is late afternoon, when the berries are dry and the sun isn't too hot.

Look, Ma, two hands!
Ask a grownup or a friend to help you tie the pail around your waist or hang it around your neck with the rope. Then you have two hands free for picking.

Pick, pick, pick
Pick the ripe berries off the plants. Eat some as you pick, and put the rest in the pail. A family or a group of friends makes quick work of a big job.

What next?
Eat fresh, or help make blueberry pancakes or muffins or a fresh raspberry pie.

FRESH RASPBERRY PIE

fresh raspberries
8-inch baked pie shell
1 cup orange juice
⅔ cup sugar
2 tablespoons corn starch

Pile the raspberries in the pie shell. Place the remaining ingredients in a saucepan. Heat and stir until the mixture reaches the boiling point and thickens. Cool. Spoon over the fresh berries in the pie shell. Cool some more. Serve with a dollop of vanilla ice cream or whipped cream. Easy as pie!

SAMPLING

▲ **Nothing beats the taste of a sun-warm strawberry. Tadhg likes this harvesting chore!**

BLUEBERRIES

▲ **Sean and his grand-father pick and eat blueberries. "One for me, one for the bucket."**

TASTE TEST

◄ **Sean and Katie harvest strawberries from their dad's garden. The best part of this job is the tasting!**

VARIATION

Help to pick ripe strawberries, too. They are scrumptious! Because they grow so close to the ground, the pail-around-the-waist method is not practical. Fill a container placed on the ground next to you.

CHAPTER 7

LET'S PLANT!
FLOWERS AND HERBS

In or out of the vegetable patch, ornamental flowers, with their splashes of bright color, will give many young gardeners pleasure. A few flowers or herbs tucked in among the vegetables will be good companions and help to repel garden pests.

Some children may enjoy tending a flower or herb garden of their own. Keep it small and simple, for quick and easy maintenance. Although vegetable patches may produce crops despite neglect, forgotten flower gardens merely look terrible, so encourage first attempts that are postage-stamp size. Depending on the age and interest of the child, plant bulbs, seed tapes, seeds started indoors or out, purchased seedlings, or divisions of perennial plants shared by neighbors and friends.

GIVE THEM GOOD SOIL

Flowers, like vegetables, thrive in well-prepared soil that contains lots of organic matter. You will have more blooms if you go easy on the nitrogen and add an extra measure of phosphorus (see Chapter 5).

Herbs are pest free, aromatic, and easy to grow. Most need a site with good drainage, not-too-rich soil, and lots of sun. Mints are an exception. They like rich, moist soil, and grow vigorously in partial shade.

STARTING A NEW BED?

Don't grunt and groan removing sod. Let it help enrich the soil. All you need to do is plan ahead. See "Abracadabra: Sod Into Soil!" on p. 40 for particulars.

MAKE FRIENDS WITH A FLOWER

Many flowers have wonderful names. Grow a few "personalities" in your own garden and introduce them to a child, or help him grow some of the easy ones in a little patch or portable pot. Learning their names is like making friends. Meet Veronica, Sweet William, Johnny-Jump-Up, and black-eyed Susan. Start a menagerie with catnip, pussytoes, lamb's ears, beebalm, hens and chickens, or snapdragons. Try forget-me-not, bleeding heart, coral bells, feverfew, four-o-clocks, candytuft, snowdrops, baby's breath, or honesty.

FLOWER CROPS

We usually think of vegetables when we think of crops, but flower gardens give us usable produce, too.

Eat them!
Let a child pick a few violets, nasturtiums, or chive blossoms to add to a green salad. Or make a tossed flower salad with blooms of borage, nasturtium, and chive. Cut daylily buds or squash blossoms just before they open and sauté lightly in butter.

Dip mint leaves, violet and borage

WHAT'S THE DIFFERENCE BETWEEN ANNUALS AND PERENNIALS?

Annuals grow, flower, produce seeds, and die all in one season. Perennials live for many years. In cold climates, the leaves and stems of many perennials die back in winter, but under the ground the roots stay alive, to sprout new growth in spring.

SPRINGTIME

▶ **Tulips and hyacinths bring spring joy to Jenny.**

COMPANIONABLE HERBS

Herb	*Companions*
Basil	Companion to tomatoes, *dislikes* rue. Repels flies and mosquitos.
Borage	Companion to tomatoes, squash, and strawberries; deters tomato worm.
Caraway	Plant here and there; loosens soil.
Catnip	Plant in borders; deters flea beetle.
Camomile	Companion to cabbages and onions.
Chervil	Companion to radishes.
Chives	Companion to carrots.
Dead Nettle	Companion to potatoes; deters potato bug.
Dill	Companion to cabbage; *dislikes* carrots.
Fennel	*Most plants dislike it;* plant away from gardens.
Flax	Companion to carrots, potatoes; deters potato bug.
Garlic	Plant near roses and raspberries; deters Japanese beetle.
Horseradish	Plant at corners of potato patch; deters potato bug.
Henbit	General insect repellent.
Hyssop	Companion to cabbage and grapes; deters cabbage moth. *Dislikes* radishes.
Marigolds	Plant throughout garden; it discourages Mexican bean beetles, nematodes, and other insects. The workhorse of companion plants.
Mint	Companion to cabbage and tomatoes; deters white cabbage moth.
Mole plant	Deters moles and mice if planted around garden.
Nasturtium	Companion to radishes, cabbage, and cucurbits; plant under fruit trees. Deters aphids, squash bugs, striped pumpkin beetles.
Petunia	Companion to beans.
Pot Marigold	Companion to tomatoes, but plant elsewhere, too. Deters tomato worm, asparagus beetles, and other pests.
Rosemary	Companion to cabbage, beans, carrots, and sage: deters cabbage moth, bean beetles, and carrot fly.
Rue	Companion to roses and raspberries; deters Japanese beetles. *Dislikes* sweet basil.
Sage	Plant with rosemary, cabbage, and carrots; *dislikes* cucumbers. Deters cabbage moth, carrot fly.
Southernwood	Companion to cabbage; deters cabbage moth.
Sowthistle	In moderate amounts, this weed can help tomatoes, onions, and corn.
Summer Savory	Companion to beans and onions; deters bean beetles.
Tansy	Plant under fruit trees; companion to roses and raspberries. Deters flying insects, Japanese beetles, striped cucumber beetles, squash bugs, and ants.
Thyme	Companion to cabbage; deters cabbage worm.
Wormwood	As a border, it keeps animals from the garden.
Yarrow	Plant along borders, paths, and near aromatic herbs; enhances production of essential oils.

blossoms, or (unsprayed) rose petals first in beaten egg white, then in super-fine sugar. Let dry on waxed paper and use to decorate a special cake.

Dry them

Hang garden or field flowers upside-down to dry and use for flower arrangements, in wreaths, or in tiny bouquets called tussie-mussies. Dried herbs and flowers are the ingredients for pot-pourri, sachets, moth repellents, bath perfume, and toys for a favorite kitten.

PLANT FOR OTHERS

Is there a youth garden club in your community? It can provide fellowship and camaraderie to accompany flower gardening activities. In our town the Junior Garden Club, with members from six to fourteen years old, has re-searched, planned, and planted a colonial herb garden at the eighteenth-century Peter Matteson Tavern; planted windowboxes and a playhouse garden at the Victorian-era Park-McCullough House; established a garden of peren-nials at a nursing home; and planted thousands of spring-flowering bulbs at many sites in the community. Young members have also learned the basics of flower arranging and have entered flower shows.

WHAT'S A FLOWER FOR?

A flower is a factory. Its product is a seed.
Some flowers even advertise for workers to help produce
the seed.

YOU NEED

- Flowers to observe
- A magnifying glass
- A piece of black construction paper
- An Exacto knife or razor blade
- A grownup to help

TIME OF YEAR

Spring and summer

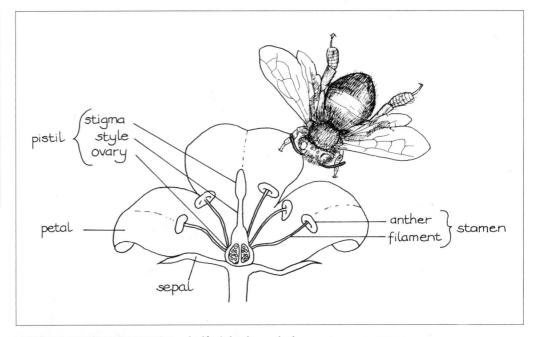

Examine a flower
Daffodils, tulips, poppies, daylilies, and lilies have large, easy-to-observe blossoms. Look for the green, leaflike sepals where the flower joins the stem. They are like a cup, holding the petals. Inside the petals are the special flower parts that produce the seed. First come the many stamens, with dust-like pollen on the anthers at their tips. In the center of the flower is the pistil. Its top, called the stigma, is sticky, to catch the pollen. Use the magnifying glass to get a close look. Shake the flower, and catch the pollen on the construction paper. Look at it through the glass.

Dissect the flower
Ask a grownup to help you carefully cut the flower in

half, right through the center of the pistil, which is the female part of the flower. Can you see the swollen ovary at the base of the pistil? Inside the chamber(s) of the ovary are tiny eggs. When pollen grains from the male stamens touch the top of the pistil, they grow tubes down the style of the pistil and fertilize the eggs in the ovary. Then the eggs develop into seeds! Your magnifying glass will help you see this tiny miracle-room better.

Wait and look again
Watch another flower of the same kind until its petals dry up and fall off. Can you see the ovary expanding? Do you think the eggs inside have changed? When the ovary looks really fat, ask a grownup to help you cut it open. What do you see? How has it changed from when

INSECTS

▲ **Bees and other insects carry pollen from the anthers of one flower to the pistil of another.**

DAFFODILS

▶ **Pistil and stamens are easy to find inside the cup of each daffodil.**

▼ **Toothwort blooms in spring woods. Its Latin name is *Dentaria diphylla*.**

THE NO-EGGPLANT YEAR

What happens to the flowers of tomatoes, eggplant, peppers, beans, peas, pumpkins, cucumbers, and squash? Nat and Alix Vander Els found out, and used their knowledge in a contrary way.

They disliked eating eggplants, so throughout the summer they stealthily removed all the blossoms from each plant.

"My plants were wonderfully healthy, but they produced no eggplants," their mom recalls. She shrugged her shoulders, and attributed the failure to the vagaries of that particular season.

Four years later, her children confessed. The family is still laughing about that no-eggplant year.

WHAT ARE FLOWERS FOR?

Flowers are for making seeds for next year's plants.

you first looked? When you eat an apple (or any other fruit), you are eating a swollen ovary, with the seeds inside. A pumpkin is a giant ovary with hundreds of huge seeds inside. Many "vegetables" are really fruits—ripened flower ovaries: tomatoes, peppers, eggplants, cucumbers, squashes, peas, beans, and corn. What about broccoli? You eat the tightly closed buds of the broccoli flower. If you wait too long before harvesting, the buds open into yellow flowers.

Many flowers in one package

Some flowers are like apartment houses. They are really many tiny flowers (called florets) packed tightly together in one flower head. These kinds of flowers are called COMPOSITES.

A sunflower is a composite. Sunflower petals surround scores of miniature florets. Each has its own set of stamens, and a pistil with an ovary. Each ovary will swell after pollination to produce one sunflower seed. Daisies, black-eyed Susans, dandelions, marigolds, asters, zinnias, cornflowers, and strawflowers are other common composites.

Seeds everywhere

Usually, flower gardeners snip off blooms when they fade, so the plant won't make seeds, because once it has formed seeds the plant's "job" in life is finished and it doesn't need to make more flowers. Let a few of your flowers "go to seed." Open the ovaries and compare the sizes and shapes of seeds produced by iris, poppies, marigolds, cornflowers, calendula, peonies, dandelions, thistles—whatever flowers grow in your garden, in the empty lot, between the cracks in the sidewalk, or in a meadow or woods.

Not all flowers produce seeds in the same way. Usually, the pollen from one flower must get to the pistil of another flower (although some flowers can fertilize themselves). How does it get there? By hitching a ride on an insect or with the wind!

Advertising

Flowers with brightly colored petals are advertising for helpers. Their petals are a landing field for the insects that work for them. Some even attract their helpers with fragrance. Bees, hummingbirds, flies, butterflies, and moths visit the flowers for nectar and, as they travel from flower to flower, they carry pollen from the anthers of one plant to the pistil of another. Without bees, we wouldn't have any apples!

No advertising

Wind is another flower helper. Flowers that are wind-pollinated may not look at all like flowers to you. They do not need to be showy to attract the wind. Corn is wind-pollinated. Its tassles are the male flowers and its silks are the female flowers' pollen receivers. Grasses and many trees and weeds are wind-pollinated. Look in spring for tree flowers that don't look like flowers at all—on pine trees, birches, oaks, and others.

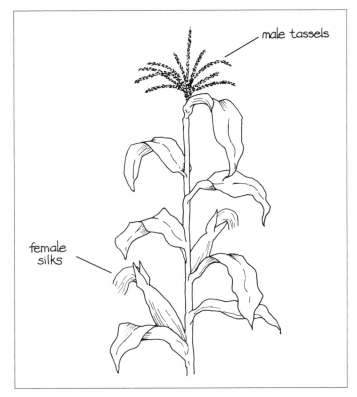

WIND

▲ **Corn is pollinated by the wind.**

GIANTS IN THE GARDEN: SUNFLOWERS AND BLACK DRAGON LILIES

YOU NEED

- A 2-foot-wide row with lots of sun, on the north side of the garden
- Compost and/or well-rotted manure
- Bone meal and wood ashes, or granite dust and lime
- Sunflower seeds
- A watering can or hose
- Manure tea, fish emul-sion, or liquid fertilizer
- Mulch
- A measuring stick or tape

WHEN TO PLANT

When danger of frost is past and the ground has warmed up

TIME TO HARVEST

Two and a half months

PLANT SUNFLOWERS

Watch these cousins of the daisy grow taller than you!

Feed the soil
Sunflowers need lots of food to grow so tall in one sum-mer! Spread 4 or more inches of well-rotted manure and/or compost on the soil. Add a sprinkling of bone meal. Add wood ashes, or granite dust and a bit of lime. Dig it in, hoe the clods, and rake the soil.

Plant the seed
Make a furrow with a hoe and drop in the seeds, about a foot apart. Cover with ½ inch of soil. Sunflowers need lots of sun. Plant them on the north side of the garden, so they don't shade other plants.

Water the seed
Soak the planting area thoroughly.

What next?
The seeds should sprout in seven to fourteen days. Pull out every other seedling, so plants are 2 feet apart. Give them lots of water, and an occasional drink of manure tea, fish emulsion, or liquid fertilizer. They're always hungry!

Mulch the soil, so you won't have to spend a lot of time weeding.

How tall?
Measure the height of your sunflowers after flowers form. Measure your own

MEASURING
▲ **Betsy holds the tape to find out how Stephanie and Katie "measure up" to this giant sunflower.**

HELLO UP THERE
◄ **Both Betsy and her sun-flower show sunny faces.**

FRIENDS AND ENEMIES

Sunflowers are good companions for corn or cucumbers. Keep them away from potatoes and beans.

Native Americans grew sunflowers, too. They ate the seeds raw, ground them into sunflower meal to use in cooking, extracted the oil to use in their hair, made yellow dye from the flower heads, and used the fibers from the stalks in weaving.

VINCENT VAN GOGH, a Dutch painter who lived 100 years ago, made wonderful sunflower paintings. Can you paint a sunflower life-size?

height. How much taller is the tallest sunflower?

Or measure the same sunflower plant every week until it's full-grown. Make a graph to show its progress.

Harvest time!
Watch the flowers grow larger and larger. They are "composites"—many flowers in one. When the petals have dropped off and the birds be-gin to peck at the outer rows of seed, cut off the heads with a foot of stalk. Hang them upside down in a dry, airy place.

Nutritious nibbles
When all the seeds are dry, rub them off the head and put them in an airtight container, for a nutritious snack for you or the birds. Who can hull a seed faster, you or a cardinal?

CLOSEUP

▲ **A sunflower is a "composite." How many florets produced these seeds?**

PLANT A BLACK DRAGON LILY

This black dragon breathes fragrance instead of fire when it blooms in July and August.

YOU NEED

- A spot with good drainage
- A spade
- Compost, well-rotted manure, and bone meal
- A Black Dragon lily bulb (or other Aurelian hybrid)
- A watering can or hose
- Mulch
- A stake (optional)

WHEN TO PLANT

Early spring or fall

Plant the bulb
Dig a big hole and enrich the soil in the hole with compost and well-rotted manure. Mix in a dollop of bone meal. Set the bulb 6 to 8 inches deep, and fill in the hole with soil.

Water and mulch
Soak the planting area well and add a blanket of mulch.

What next?
Roots will grow out of the stalk above the bulb. Water if the weather is dry. By mid-summer, you will have a tall plant with fragrant blossoms, white on the inside and dark red on the outside. Stake, if necessary, but Black Dragons are pretty sturdy on their own. Say, "Hi, Black Dragon," and smell its perfume.

Black Dragon Lily

GIANT

▲ **A Black Dragon lily is a fragrant giant in the garden.**

PLANT SPRING-FLOWERING BULBS

Plant spring joy in fall, an easy project with big rewards.

Prepare the soil
Dig some compost or well-rotted (not fresh!) manure into the soil. Choose a spot in light shade, where the bulbs won't be disturbed by cultivation in summer.

What bulbs will you plant?
■ SNOWDROPS are early bloomers. Their tiny white flowers, true harbingers of spring, poke up through melting snow.

■ DAFFODILS are dependable. The bulbs are bitter, so you don't have to worry about hungry squirrels, mice, and chipmunks devouring them. They'll bloom for many years.

■ Rodents think TULIPS are sweet and delectable. To discourage tulip feasts, plant a bulb or two of FRITILLARIA IMPERIALIS with a group of tulips. These stately plants with umbrella-like blossoms emit a skunk-like odor that repels nibbling creatures.

How deep? How far apart?
Little bulbs such as snowdrops should be planted 3 inches deep and 3 inches apart. Daffodils and tulips should go down 6 or more inches, about 6 inches apart; and the large bulbs of Fritillaria imperialis should be at least 7 inches deep. (In warm climates, plant everything 4 inches deeper).

Photo by Linda Tilgner

Plant them
Dig a hole with a trowel, mix a spoonful of bone meal into the soil at the bottom of the hole, and place a bulb in firm contact with soil, roots down, tip up. Fill in the hole with soil.

Add water and a blanket
Soak well and mulch with wood chips, chopped leaves, straw, pine needles, evergreen branches, shredded sugar cane, or the like.

Wait till spring
Watch for tips of green to poke out of the ground. Add a sprinkling of bone meal or garden fertilizer to the soil. When bulbs bloom, cut a few to bring indoors to make you joyful. Watch the tight buds of snowdrop open in the cozy warmth of a house,

and look for the delicate green markings inside the blossom.

What next?
When flowers fade, snip them off; don't let them go to seed. Leaves, however, are factories to build strength for next year's flowers. Leave them undisturbed until they turn yellow and disappear. Then, like magic, they'll emerge again next year, shouting, "Hooray for spring!"

WHAT IS A BULB?

A bulb is an underground bud. Inside is a package of leaves, stem, food, and sleeping roots. Onions, lilies, daffodils, and tulips are some of the plants we grow from bulbs.

YOU NEED

■ A patch of ground with good drainage
■ Compost or well-rotted manure
■ Bone meal
■ A trowel
■ Spring-flowering bulbs:
Snowdrops
Daffodils
Tulips and fritillaria imperialis
■ A watering can or hose
■ Mulch
■ Garden labels

WHEN TO PLANT

Early fall

WELCOME SIGHT

▲ **Snowdrops are among the earliest bulbs to bloom.**

SPRINGTIME

▶ **Will planted these daffodils last fall.**

FOUR SIMPLE FLOWER AND HERB GARDENS

For a young child a tiny patch of annuals, a cascade of sweet peas, or an assortment of mints confined by sunken flue tiles provide quick results with minimum effort and maintenance. A drying garden is a natural for an older child with an interest in flower arranging. Most ambitious is the fragrance garden, source of potpourri, which is suggested as a joint parent-child project, or as a group undertaking with adult help and guidance. Both the mint garden and the fragrance garden provide sensory stimulation for a visually handicapped child, who can help with the planting or merely enjoy scents and textures as the garden matures.

EASY-TO-GROW ANNUALS MAKE A MINI FLOWER GARDEN

A bright patch of yellow, orange, blue, and white gives pleasure all summer.

YOU NEED

- A 2-foot by 4-foot sunny patch of garden
- Landscaping boards to frame it (optional)
- A spade, hoe, rake, and trowel
- Compost, bone meal, and wood ashes (or granite dust)
- Seeds or seedlings for:
  8 white sweet alyssum
  6 dwarf orange or bi-color marigolds
  3 tall yellow hybrid marigolds
  3 blue cornflowers
- Liquid fertilizer
- A watering can or hose

WHEN TO PLANT

Spring

Prepare the plot
Spread 2 to 3 inches of compost and a sprinkling of bone meal and wood ashes on the soil. Dig it in, hoe the clods, and rake smooth. For easiest maintenance, have an adult enclose the area with landscaping boards, to make a raised bed.

Seeds or plants?
- SEEDLINGS. The least-work way is to buy seedlings

VARIATION: PLANT A CASCADE OF SWEET PEAS

Grow these cool-weather climbers on a fence, trellis, or netting in the vegetable garden or behind a flower garden.

YOU NEED

- A pea fence, trellis, or netting 6 or more feet high
- Compost, bone meal, and wood ashes
- A spade, hoe, and rake
- Sweet pea seeds
- A watering can or hose
- Mulch

WHEN TO PLANT

As early in the spring as the ground can be worked

Feed the soil
Spread compost and a sprinkling of bone meal and wood ashes on the soil, dig it in, hoe the clods, and rake smooth.

A place to climb
Erect the pea fence, or install poles and netting (unless you are using a trellis already in place).

This is a two-person job.

Plant the sweet peas
Soak the seeds overnight. (Remember that sweet pea seeds are poisonous and should not be eaten!) Make a furrow with the hoe, and drop in the seeds, about 3 inches apart. Cover with about an inch of soil.

Water, water, water, and mulch
Sweet peas like cool weather and lots of water. Water after planting and don't ever let them get thirsty. Mulch to keep roots cool. Watch them climb higher and higher.

Sniff and snip
Enjoy the fragrance of the blossoms (the old-fashioned varieties are the most sweetly scented) and keep snipping the blooms. They are wonderful bouquets for the house. Never let even one pea pod form, or the vines will think their job is done, and will stop making more flowers.

from a nursery or flower market and set them in place when danger of frost is past. Make sure the seedlings have been hardened off, or postpone planting for a week while you do it (see p. 51). If seedlings are in plant trays, slice between them with a knife to get roots and soil ready to move in a solid cube.

Before planting, space the seedlings in the plot according to the plan. With a trowel, dig a small hole for each seedling, so that it is set at the same level it was growing. Set each plant in a hole and firm soil around it. Settle the roots and give the plants a boost by watering with a trickle of half-strength liquid fertilizer.

If you are more ambitious, you can start your own seedlings indoors six to eight weeks before the last frost (see p. 48). Be meticulous about cleanliness, as sweet alyssum seedlings are susceptible to damping off.

■ SEEDS. Plant cornflowers and sweet alyssum directly in the garden in early spring. Drop a small pinch of seeds in each planting location, cover with fine soil, and mark each spot with a little stick. Water well with a fine spray. No need to thin, as the plants are spindly and can grow together.

Wait until danger of frost is past before planting the marigolds in the same way. When seedlings have two true leaves, snip off all but the strongest plant in each spot.

MARIGOLDS

▲ Sean and Lindsey set marigold seedlings in their raised flower bed.

◄ Planting plan, Mini Flower Garden

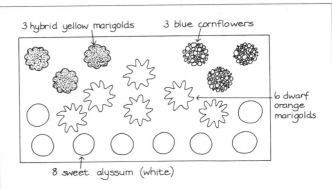

3 hybrid yellow marigolds

3 blue cornflowers

6 dwarf orange marigolds

8 sweet alyssum (white)

▶ **"Cheers!" say Ben, Ny, and Vy, enjoying mint lemonade.**

VARIATION: PLANT YOUR INITIALS

Watch your initials bloom against a white background!

YOU NEED

- A 2-foot by 4-foot plot of garden
- Landscaping boards (optional)
- A spade, hoe, and rake
- Compost, bone meal, and wood ashes (or granite dust)
- One 15-foot seed tape for orange or bicolored dwarf marigolds
- Sweet alyssum seed

- A watering can or hose

WHEN TO PLANT

After danger of frost is past

Plant, water, and wait! Prepare the soil in the same way. Make a furrow in the shape of your initials. Lay the dwarf marigold seed tape in the furrow, and cover with fine soil. Sprinkle sweet alyssum seeds thinly in the empty spaces. Cover lightly with soil, tamp down, and moisten with a fine spray of water.

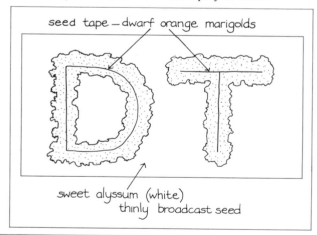

seed tape — dwarf orange marigolds

sweet alyssum (white) thinly broadcast seed

Pamper the babies
Keep your garden weeded until the plants get sturdy. Keep the soil moist but not sodden. Then mulch with a seed-free layer of mulch to save work.

Enjoy the show!
Snip off dead blooms, and each plant will make more

and more flowers. Trim sweet alyssum with a scissors now and then. It's like giving it a haircut!

Substitutions
Other easy-to-grow annuals include nasturtiums, zinnias, dwarf dahlias, calendula, cosmos, and asters.

YOU NEED

- 5 square flue tiles*
- 1 round flue tile*
  * (Look for tiles at bargain prices.)
- A well-drained patch of garden, about 3½ feet by 2¼ feet, in sun or partial shade
- A spade, cultivator, and trowel
- A grownup
- Sand, peat moss, compost, and lime
- One plant each of:
  spearmint
  peppermint
  apple mint
  or English mint
  orange mint
  or pineapple mint
  lemon balm
  catnip
- A few pieces of wooly thyme (optional)
- A watering can or hose
- Shredded bark or wood chips

WHEN TO PLANT

Early spring

PLANT A MINT GARDEN

You need a grownup to help you sink the flue tiles in the garden. After that, it's easy as pie!

Construct the garden
It's a lot of work to sink the flue tiles in the garden so the tops are level with the soil, but it's worth the effort. Without some restraint, mints spread madly. Fencing in the roots means you'll never have to worry about runaway mint. Following the plan, sink three square flue tiles in the back and sink the circular tile between the other two squares in the front.

Fill the flue tiles
Fill each tile with a mixture of soil, sand, peat moss, compost, and lime. No fresh manure, please! It can cause a disease called rust, to which mints are particularly susceptible.

Plant the garden
Where do you get the plants? Anyone who has mint will gladly share a piece with you. Or you can buy small plants at a garden center or through a catalog. Place each plant in its tile, according to the diagram, firm soil around the roots, and water well.

Mulch the spaces
Spread wood chips, shredded bark, or the like between the flue tiles. If you like, plant a few pieces of wooly thyme between the tiles.

MAKE MINT LEMONADE

Crush a handful of mint and lemon balm leaves. Place in the bottom of a quart pitcher. Pour 2 cups of boiling water over the leaves, and add 4 spoonfuls of honey. Let steep for 15 minutes. Stir vigorously, remove the leaves, add the juice of a lemon, and fill the pitcher with ice cubes. Garnish with sprigs of mint, and sip refreshing coolness on a hot summer day.

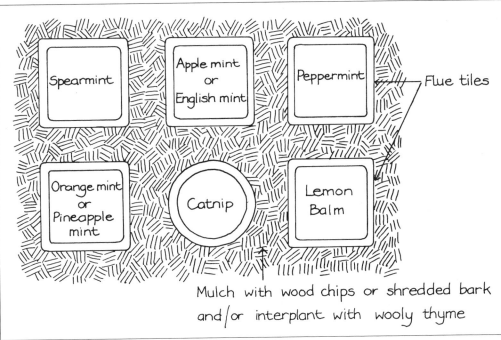

Spearmint

Apple mint or English mint

Peppermint

Flue tiles

Orange mint or Pineapple mint

Catnip

Lemon Balm

Mulch with wood chips or shredded bark and/or interplant with wooly thyme

▲ **Planting plan, Mint Garden**

MAKE A CATNIP MOUSE

Stuff a fabric mouse with dried catnip. Your cat will love this special toy.

Fold a piece of sturdy, close-weave fabric in half, with right sides together. Trace and cut out the body, tail, and ears.

Position the tail in place between the pieces, so it will be attached when you sew the outer seam of the body. Stitch the body together by machine or with tiny hand stitches, ¼ inch from the edge, leaving an open space at the bottom for stuffing.

Turn the body inside out, stuff with dried catnip leaves, and stitch up the bottom. Sew on ears and beady eyes, and add a nose and whiskers with heavy thread.

Pattern for catnip mouse

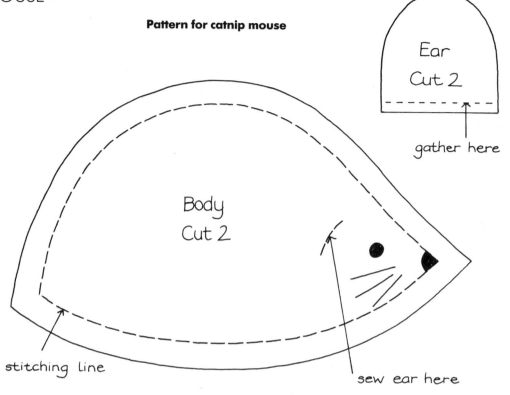

Ear
Cut 2

gather here

Body
Cut 2

stitching line

sew ear here

Tail Cut 1

CAT'S FAVORITE

▼ **A catnip mouse is a favorite toy for a feline friend.**

Mini-weeding
Keep weeds out of the center of each tile. Keep the soil moist until roots are established. The mints will fill in quickly. During the summer, cut them back to ground level and fresh new stalks will spring up.

Use them fresh
Garnish iced tea with sprigs of fresh mint or lemon balm. Add perky mint leaves to fruit salads. Use sprays of mint as fillers in flower arrangements, too.

Use them dry
■ A WINTER'S SUPPLY. To dry catnip, lemon balm, and the mints, cut the stems just before the plant flowers, after the morning dew has dried but before the sun gets hot. Tie in small bunches, and hang upside-down out of the sun, in a dry, airy place. When are they dry enough? When leaves are crackly like cornflakes!

■ HOT TEA. Strip the leaves off the stems, put them in small jars, and make fancy labels. Make mint or catnip tea by putting a spoonful of the dried leaves in a tea ball. Pour boiling water over it and steep for 5 to 10 minutes. Add honey to taste.

SQUARE STEMS, OPPOSITE LEAVES

All the plants in this garden are members of the mint family. How can you tell? Examine a stem. It's square! Look at the arrangement of leaves. They grow opposite one another.

(A volatile oil gives mints their special fragrance. Look for the tiny oil-producing glands on leaves and stems.)

PLANT A DRYING GARDEN

From this gay summer garden, harvest flowers to dry for winter bouquets.

Prepare the soil

Dig a goodly amount of sand (if your soil is heavy) and some lime and bone meal into the soil. These plants don't like a lot of manure. Hoe the clods and rake smooth. If you like, enclose the garden with treated landscaping boards.

Plant the perennials

Lay out the plants according to the garden plan. With a trowel, dig a small hole for each plant, set it at the same level it was growing, and firm the soil around it. Put extra lime in the soil in and around the baby's breath. Trickle a half-strength solution of liquid fertilizer around each plant, to settle soil and give the seedling a good start.

Avoid sprawl

Make a cylinder out of the coated fencing, slip it over the baby's breath, and anchor it in the back with a small stake. As the baby's breath grows, it will poke through the holes in the fencing and hide it. The cylinder will keep the plant from sprawling.

Plant the annuals

When danger of frost is past, sow the seeds for globe amaranth and strawflower di-

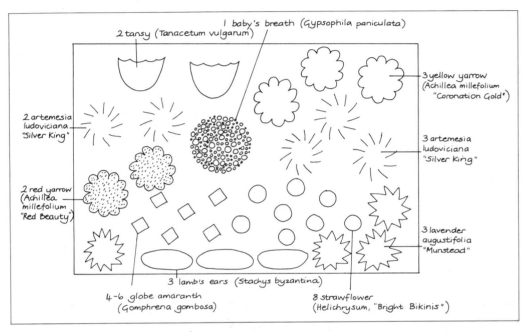

▲ Planting plan, Drying Garden.

1 baby's breath (Gypsophila paniculata)
2 tansy (Tanacetum vulgarum)
2 artemesia ludoviciana "Silver King"
2 red yarrow (Achillea millefolium "Red Beauty")
3 yellow yarrow (Achillea millefolium "Coronation Gold")
3 artemesia ludoviciana "Silver King"
3 lavender augustifolia "Munstead"
3 lamb's ears (Stachys byzantina)
4-6 globe amaranth (Gomphrena gombosa)
8 strawflower (Helichrysum, "Bright Bikinis")

YOU NEED

- A 4-foot by 6-foot sunny, well-drained patch of garden
- Landscaping boards to enclose it (optional)
- Sand, lime, bone meal
- A spade, hoe, rake, and trowel
- Perennial seedlings or divisions:
  2 tansy
  3 yellow yarrow ("Coronation Gold")
  2 red yarrow ("Red Beauty")
  5 *Artemisia ludoviciana,* "Silver King"
  1 baby's breath
  4 lavender ("Munstead")
  3 lamb's ears
- Annual seeds or seedlings:
  4 to **6** globe amaranth
  8 strawflower ("Bright Bikinis")
- A cylinder of green plastic-coated wire pea fencing, 18 inches high by 3 feet long
- A stake
- A watering can or hose
- Liquid fertilizer

WHEN TO PLANT

Spring

rectly in the garden. Thin to about 8 inches apart.

What next?
Keep the garden watered and weeded while plants are small. When they are well-established, mulch if you like. Enjoy the bright colors!

Harvest and dry
Harvest with a foot or more of stem just before flowers are fully open. This could be as early as July for the yarrow. Wait until after September first before cutting the artemisia . If you cut it too early, it will turn an ugly gray. If you wait, it will stay a lovely silvery color.

See directions for drying on p. 110.

What for?
Use the dried flowers for

winter bouquets, or to add to artemisia, straw, and grape-vine wreaths. Make lavender sachets out of its dried leaves and flowers. Burn the dry stems of lavender in your wood stove for a pleasing fragrance.

TANSY TIPS

Tansy spreads. Cut into the soil around it every spring. In colonial times, women put a sprig of tansy in the kitchen cup-board to keep moths out of the flour. Dried leaves of tansy, southernwood, and santolina can be sewn inside small fabric bags and hung on hangers in a closet to repel moths.

BUNCHES

▲ (TOP) Dorothy Dunn advises Katie as she ties a bunch of stripped stems together.

GOLDEN

▲ (BOTTOM) Yellow yarrow (*Achillea "Coronation Gold"*) has strong, stiff stems and retains its golden color after drying.

PLANT A POTPOURRI GARDEN: FRAGRANCE THAT LASTS

Lavender and an old-fashioned rose form the backbone of this garden. It's O.K. to step on the edging of thyme and scented geraniums, to bring out the fragrance of their leaves. Stepping stones make the rest of the garden accessible for sniffing. All the plants can be dried to use in sachets and potpourri.

Plant the rose

The hole for a rosebush should be prepared in the same way as the hole for a dwarf fruit tree (see p. 118)—big, and rich! Keep the rosebush in a bucket of water until you're ready to plant.

Make a mound of enriched soil in the bottom of the hole. Trim off broken roots, and any too long to fit in the hole.

Arrange the rosebush roots over the mound of soil, so that the bud union (the bulge that shows where the top was grafted to the rootstock) is at ground level (if you live in a warm climate), or 2 inches below (if you live in a place with cold winters). Fill the hole two-thirds full with rich soil. Tamp down and water well. Then add the rest of the soil, plus some extra to make a hill that buries the top 6 to 8 inches of rosebush. Water again.

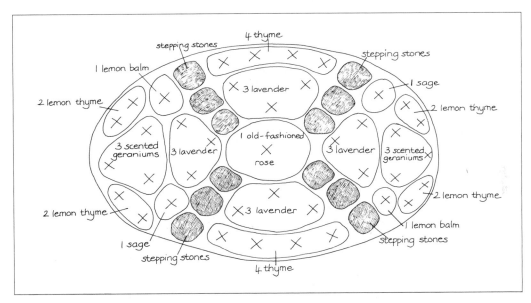

▲ Planting plan, Potpourri Garden

YOU NEED

- An old-fashioned, fragrant rosebush: possibilities are damask rose, moss rose, rugosa rose, and, in warmer areas, a hybrid perpetual or a bourbon rose
- A spade, hoe, rake, and trowel
- Compost and well-rotted manure
- Sand, lime, and bone meal
- Sharp knife or pruning shears
- Stepping stones
- Seedlings (buy them or start your own):
  12 lavender
  8 thyme
  8 lemon thyme
  2 sage
  2 lemon balm
- **6** scented geraniums: choose from those with leaves that smell like rose, lemon, peppermint, nutmeg, orange, pine, eucalyptus, or spice
- A watering can or hose
- Mulch

WHEN TO PLANT

Early spring (or fall if you live where winters are mild)

FRAGRANT

▼ **Allyson enjoys the fragrance of a rose before separating the petals to dry for potpourri.**

The hill of soil keeps the canes from drying out while the roots start to grow. Remove the soil covering the canes gradually as days go by and leaves begin to sprout.

Feed the soil
Spread sand, compost, and bone meal on the rest of the garden. Dig in, hoe the clods, and rake smooth.

Step here, please!
Lay the stepping stones in the garden according to the plan.

Plant the herbs
Place the lavender, thymes, sage, and lemon balm seedlings in the garden according to the plan. Water well. Wait until frost danger is past before setting out the scented geraniums.

Save weeding
Mulch with shredded bark, shredded sugar cane, cocoa bean hull, or the like to cut down on weeding chores.

Winter care
Before the first killing frost, pot up the scented geraniums and find them a cool but sunny spot inside the house for the winter.

Right after the first killing frost, pile soil 8 to 10 inches high around the canes of the rosebush. Bring in soil from another place to make this protective mound. If you try to dig it from the garden, you may disturb roots of the resident rose and herbs.

OTHER FRAGRANT FLOWERS

Many flowers have lovely fragrance. Grow some of these, or look for them in someone else's garden, and enjoy the delicate perfume.

Annuals and biennials
Sweet William
nicotiana
sweet alyssum
sweet pea
white petunia
heliotrope
wallflower
herbs

Perennials
peony
valerian
gas plant
monarda didyma
phlox
herbs
sweet violet

Bulbs, corms, tubers
daylily (lemon lily and hyperion)
lily
poeticus narcissi
hyacinth
lily-of-the-valley

Shrubs, trees, and vines
jasmine
wisteria
lilac
viburnum
mock-orange
mimosa
spice bush
daphne
gardenia, camellia
orange
apple

MAKE POTPOURRI

YOU NEED

- Flower shears
- Rose buds and petals
- Lavender flowers
- Leaves of rose geranium (or other scented geraniums) (optional)
- Leaves of lemon balm (optional)
- An old screen set up on blocks in a dark, dry, and airy place
- Gum benzoin powder (available from a pharmacy or a potpourri supplier)
- Vanilla beans (find them in the spice department of the food store)
- Ground allspice
- Ground cloves
- A tiny bit of oil of lavender or oil of roses (optional)
- A large jar with cover

TIME OF YEAR

Early summer

Collect the flowers
Cut them in the morning, after the dew has dried, but before the sun gets hot.

Dry the flowers
Leave some rosebuds whole. Pick apart the petals of opened roses. Spread the collected leaves and flowers on the screen and place it in a dark, dry, and airy place. Stir occasionally. Leave them until they are crispy dry.

Blend and cure
Mix 8 cups dried rose petals and buds with 4 cups dried lavender flowers and some dried leaves of scented geraniums and lemon balm. Add ⅔ cup gum benzoin powder and a few vanilla beans (these are fixatives, which help the flowers keep their fragrance longer).
Combine with 4 tablespoons allspice and 4 tablespoons ground cloves. Add a couple of drops of oil of lavender or oil of roses (optional).
Mix everything well, put in a large jar or jars, and set aside to "cure" for six weeks in a warm, dark, dry place. Shake occasionally.

Mmm!
Pour the finished potpourri into bowls and let it make your rooms smell wonderful!

Variation
Dry any combination of flowers and scented leaves from this garden (especially lavender), crush them, and make sachets. Cut 6-inch-diameter circles of cloth with pinking shears, put a dollop of dried fragrance in the center, draw up the sides and tie with a ribbon. To be really fancy, stitch a border of lace on the edge of the circle before you add the herbs. Give as a gift, or place in your top drawer.

If you live in a climate where the temperature does not drop below 0°F in winter, the mound of soil will be protection enough against winter chill. If you live in a colder climate, pile hay, straw, or strawy manure over the mounded canes. Keep it from blowing or washing away by topping it with a few shovelsful of soil.
Carefully remove covering and soil from the rose in spring when danger of severe frost is past.

GROW IT IN A TUB

You can grow some kind of anything in a tub outdoors: flowers, vegetables, herbs, or even a dwarf tree!

YOU NEED

- A spot with sun for several hours a day
- A container with good drainage
- Soil-less planting mix
- Seeds or seedlings
- A trowel and hand cultivator
- A watering can or hose
- Liquid fertilizer

TIME OF YEAR

The outdoor growing season

If garden space is at a premium, or if you've none at all, outdoor container growing is for you. It's a perfect project—small in scale and easy to water and watch grow, with no weeding headaches.

Choose a spot
A patio, a front porch, a stoop, a fire escape, a window ledge, a balcony, a roof—any could be a location for an outdoor container. Pick a site that has sun for several hours a day, and protection from strong winds.

Choose a container
Use your imagination. A container can be as conventional as a large flower pot, or as simple as a sturdy cardboard box lined with a heavy plastic garbage bag. Plant in a half barrel, a stoneware crock, a wooden vegetable crate, a bucket, a cast-off tree container scavenged from a nursery, or a windowbox. You can even fill a plastic trash bag with planting mix, secure the opening with a twist tie, lay it on its side, slit the top, and plant right in it!

The container should be at least 6 inches deep. It's better to have one too large than too small. Good drainage is a must. Drainage holes in the bottom of the container are best. An alternative is to put a 1-inch layer of pebbles, stones, or crockery in the bottom. You can place a large flower pot set on pebbles inside an attractive outer container, and pack the space between with peat moss or sphagnum moss. Wooden containers should have an air space underneath. Add feet, or place them on a couple of bricks.

Fill with planting mix
To eliminate the worries of soil-borne disease and weed seeds, use a soil-less planting mix. It weighs little, an added bonus if you have to carry it up steps in an apartment building. It is very dry and fluffy, and contains fertilizer to last about three weeks. After that, you will have to fertilize weekly.

Mix with water to moisten, and fill the container to within an inch or two of the rim. (If you are using a wooden container, soak it in water before adding planting mix. Otherwise, it may draw moisture from the mix, creating an air space. Then when you water, the water will run down the air space without soaking plant roots.)

Decide what to plant
- FLOWERS. Try easy-to-grow annuals, scented geraniums, or a tall, fragrant Madonna or Black Dragon lily. Start your own seedlings indoors (see p. 48), plant seeds directly in the container and thin after germination, or plant purchased seedlings. Try a combination of flowers: marigolds and sweet alyssum, geraniums and lobelia, or zinnias and ageratum. Impatiens or begonias will flower in partial shade.
- VEGETABLES. Compact tomato plants, such as Pixie, Tiny Tim, or Patio are suitable for pots. Grow lettuces, spinach, or swiss chard. Plant root crops, such as radishes, beets, or short-rooted carrots (baby french fingerlings or blunt-rooted types designed for heavy soils). Create a small pole bean tepee (see p. 72)—this one won't be large enough to

crawl inside—and combine it with annual heliotrope and ageratum.

■ HERBS. Grow kitchen herbs from seed, or plant seedlings. Try parsley, basil, chive, and thyme (see p. 190). Grow a pot of mint or lemon balm to use for cool drinks and teas. Make an all-kinds-of-herbs garden by planting each pocket of a strawberry jar with a different kind of culinary herb.

■ TREES. Grow an extra-dwarf fruit tree in a large tub (see p. 118). It needs an ample container—at least 2 feet wide and 1½ feet deep. Put the container on casters or a dolly for easy moving. Dwarf citrus can be moved indoors during northern winters, since it can bear the lack of humidity indoors. (Deciduous fruit trees such as peaches grown in outdoor containers need to be moved to a garage or shed during the winter. They don't like dry indoor atmospheres.)

Care for a tubbed plant
Check the soil for dryness daily. Regular watering and weekly fertilizing with fish emulsion or an all-purpose liquid fertilizer are important. Plants in pots dry out quickly on summer days. Keep dead flower buds picked off, shear herbs occasionally (and use the clippings in the kitchen), and harvest vegetables promptly. Enjoy!

COLORFUL

▲ **A tub of flowers looks wonderful in a yard, on a porch, or on a balcony.**

FLOWER ART

Flower arranging is an art, and the guidelines for creating a pleasing arrangement are similar to those for painting or sculpture.

YOU NEED

- Fresh flowers and foliage
- Sharp shears or clippers
- A bucket of warm water
- A block of Oasis [floral foam for fresh flowers] (available from florists)
- A sharp knife
- Water and a bowl
- 3 roofing nails and a bit of florist's clay *or* a pin holder, florist's clay, and a small piece of nylon stocking *or* adhesive florist's tape
- A low, round container for the arrangement
- A lazy susan (optional)

TIME OF YEAR

Any time

MAKE A FRESH FLOWER BOUQUET

Bring the gaiety of the outdoors inside.

Snip, snip, snip
Plan ahead. Gather flowers in early morning or late afternoon, several hours before you make the arrangement. Cut flower stems at an angle, and plunge them immediately into the warm water in the bucket. Cut stems of foliage to use in and around the flowers.

Place the bucket in a cool, dark place, such as a basement, for several hours or overnight. During this time, the flowers and foliage absorb lots of water, and are "conditioned" so that they will stay fresh a long time in your arrangement. No sense going to all the trouble of making a pretty centerpiece only to have the flowers wilt two hours later!

Mechanics: a flower arranging secret
It's like discovering a secret world when you learn the tricks to making flowers stay in place. One of the easiest methods is to use a block of Oasis, available at florist's shops. With a knife, cut a piece big enough to fill your container and come up above it about an inch. Soak it in a bowl of water while the flowers are conditioning.

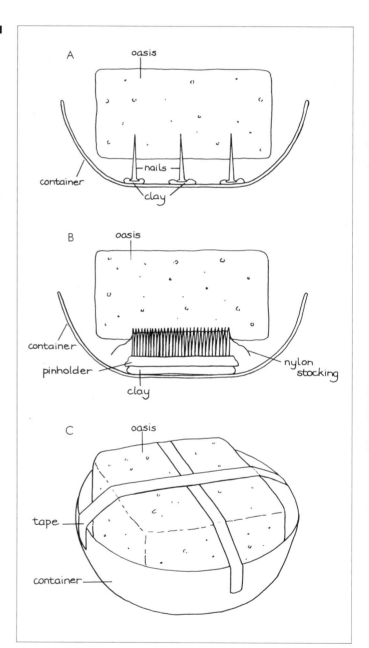

▲ **Three methods for anchoring oasis: roofing nails and florist's clay (A), pinholder and florist's clay (B), and (C), florist's tape.**

Anchor the Oasis
Keep the Oasis in place in one of these ways:

■ Put a blob of florist's clay on the head of each of three roofing nails. Press the nails, points up, on the bottom of the DRY container (If it is wet, the clay won't stick.). Push the wet Oasis onto the points of the nails.

■ Put a bit of florist's clay under a pinholder and press it firmly on the bottom of the container. Stretch a small piece of nylon stocking over the points of the holder. (It makes the Oasis easy to lift off later, without clogging the pins.) Push the Oasis down firmly onto the points of the pinholder.

■ Put the Oasis in the container. Stretch a piece of adhesive florist's tape over the Oasis so that the ends are stuck to the rim of the container. Stretch a second piece perpendicular to the first, forming a cross.

Begin with foliage
Set the container on the lazy susan, so you can turn it to see all sides. Use the greens to form the basic shape of the bouquet, to show how tall and wide it will be. Snip off the stems to make them the right length, strip off extra leaves, push stems into the Oasis, and voila! They will stay where you put them. Start with a sprig at each of the four corners, and another in the center to set the height of the arrangement. Fill in the large spaces, and point a few pieces at a downward angle to cover the Oasis. The

JUST SO

▲ Geri Thompson, advisor to the local junior garden club, counsels Katie and Stephanie on the placement of a flower in their arrangement.

ARRANGE A BASKET OF DRIED FLOWERS

Dry flowers from the garden or fields, to keep a remembrance of summer all winter.

Cut them
Harvest flowers for drying just before they are fully opened. See list for suggestions for what to look for during the season. Pick on a dry day, and wait until the dew dries in the morning. Snip before the sun saps your strength and the flowers'.

Cut the flower with a foot or more of stem. Carefully strip off the leaves. Tie in small bunches with a piece of twine or a rubber band.

Dry them
Hang the bunches upside-down in a dry, airy place out of the sun. In two to four weeks, they should be dry and crisp.

Replace some stems
Most recommended flowers have sturdy stems when dried. Strawflowers and cockscomb must have their spindly stems replaced with florist's wire.

Cut off the stem close to the base of the flower. Slip a piece of florist's wire through the center of the flower. Make a little hook on the end, so it will catch on the flower as you pull it through.

Make the arrangement
■ MECHANICS FIRST. Anchor the dry Oasis in the basket in any of the three ways sug-

gested for a fresh flower arrangement (p. 108). Place it on the lazy susan, so you can turn it as you work.

■ SKELETON NEXT. Use feathery material, such as baby's breath, to form the basic shape of the arrangement. Dried foliage of lamb's ears is good for covering the Oasis. Artemisia and pearly everlasting add variations in texture.

■ FILL IN WITH COLOR. Use globe amaranth, yarrow, strawflowers, tansy, goldenrod, or any of the other flowers on the list.

■ ENJOY! The colors of the flowers will last longer if you keep the arrangement out of sunlight and away from heat.

OASIS

▲ **A block of Oasis keeps flower stems in place and holds water to help them stay fresh.**

arrangement should be about one and a half times as wide as a low container or one and a half times as high as a tall one.

Add flowers
Foliage is the "skeleton" of the arrangement. Add the "flesh" with flowers. Place the largest flowers with the most brilliant colors low rather than high. Add the more delicate flowers to fill in. Keep turning the arrangement, to look at it from all angles. You're sculpting with flowers!

Enjoy!
Your flower sculpture should bring cheer to all for several days. If the Oasis begins to dry out, add more water.

YOU NEED

- Flowers from your drying garden or a meadow (see list)
- Sharp shears or clippers
- Twine or rubber bands
- A clothesline or rod from which to hang drying flowers
- A dry, airy place away from sunlight
- Florist's wire and wire cutters (optional)
- A basket for the arrangement
- A block of brown Oasis specifically for dried arrangements
- An anchor for the Oasis (see fresh flower bouquet directions)
- A lazy susan (optional)

TIME OF YEAR

Summer for cutting. Fall or winter for arranging.

PERFECT

▲ **Betsy puts the finishing touches on a dried arrangement.**

DRYING

◄ **With help from Betsy, Dorothy Dunn hangs a bunch of tansy to dry in the keeping room of the Peter Matteson Tavern.**

FLOWERS FOR DRYING

Grow flowers for drying in your garden or gather them from fields and roadsides. All the flowers below can be dried by hanging upside-down.

Garden Flowers
chive flowers
astilbe
coral bells
yarrow
baby's breath
lamb's ears
lavender
globe amaranth
globe thistle
cockscomb
statice
silver artemisia
iris and poppy seed pods
strawflower
honesty

hydrangea (when pink)
corn tassels

Wild Flowers
white yarrow
grasses
cattails
black-eyed Susan
goldenrod
tansy
Joe-pye-weed
pearly everlasting
grains
bittersweet
milkweed pods

In spring, gather the fertile fronds of ostrich and sensitive fern, and pussy willows. Later, cut dock, green or brown. None of these needs to be hung to dry; just store them upright in cans.

MAKE A TUG-OF-WAR WREATH

Tug and pull, to harvest grapevines twined around trees and shrubs. Children as young as seven can twist them into a wreath, and decorate it with ribbons and dried flowers or seed pods.

Harvest the grapevines
Find a place where grapevines grow. They love to climb up and over a hedgerow, or twine around trees at the edge of woods. Get permission from the owner before you grab a vine and pull! Ask a friend to help. When you've tugged out as much as you can, have an adult clip the vine.

Harvest a few vines, then remove any leaves that still cling to them. Leave tendrils on the vine. They'll add a nice touch to the finished wreath.

Form the wreath
Turn the bucket upside-down. Wrap the heaviest part of the vine in a circle around it. Lift it off the bucket and twist the rest of the vine around and around, in and out of itself, as you turn the circle. Keep adding vines, threading them in and out, weaving in protruding shoots, until the wreath is as thick as you want it to be. If you have used thick vines, it may hold its own shape. If you have used thin vines, you may need to tie the vine together in three to five places with jute or wire.

YOU NEED
- Grapevines
- Clippers
- A bucket
- Natural jute twine or wire (optional)
- Scissors
- Ribbon
- Dried flowers, seed pods, or nuts

TIME OF YEAR
Fall, after frost

CIRCLE
▶ **It's beginning to look like a wreath!**

Decorate the wreath
Twist a ribbon around the wreath, add a bow in a muted color, interweave bittersweet vines with their orange berries, or add small groups of seed pods, nuts, or dried flowers to the wreath. Added decorations look best if they are put in an odd number of places: one, three, five, or seven. Choose simple, natural decorations that will harmonize with the roughness of the grapevine.

VARIATIONS

■ Make tiny grapevine wreaths to hang on the Christmas tree. Use an inverted mug instead of a bucket as a form.

■ Make a wreath from artemisia harvested from your drying garden. Coax it into circular form by laying it to dry against the inside walls of bushel baskets. When it is dry, wire several bunches to a wire ring, overlapping to cover the wire. Decorate with dried flowers or seed pods.

GRAPEVINES
▲ Perri and Marie start their wreath by wrapping grapevines around an inverted bucket.

FINISHED
▶ Dried flowers and ribbon finish the wreath.

CHAPTER 8

LET'S PLANT! TREES

A place for a tree can be as small as a pot on a city terrace or as large as a field for a Christmas tree farm. You can even grow a tree indoors! Trees are exciting for children to plant because they grow mammoth in time. A tree's life becomes a history that parallels the life of the child.

When my sons were four and six, we transplanted foot-high white pine volunteers from a neighbor's field to our yard. Jumping over one of the tiny trees was the requisite for scoring a touchdown in backyard football games. Now, more than twenty years later, they tower over this two-story house, forming a dense grove thickly carpeted with soft needles. When I look at the giants, I still see David or Chips jumping over one, cheering for a goal scored.

FRUIT

▲ **Karyn's dwarf citrus has formed a small fruit.**

TREE PLANTING

◄ **Mike inserts a tree seedling into a hole. He checks to see that the roots are extended and that the tree is set at the same depth it grew in the nursery.**

PLANT A DWARF FRUIT TREE

A dwarf fruit tree takes up little space, fruits within a year or two of planting, and bears its fruit within easy reach for young pickers.

YOU NEED

- A spot with good air circulation and good drainage
- A spade or shovel
- Compost, manure, and/or other organic materials
- A tarp
- A dwarf fruit tree
- A bucket of water
- A hose and a water supply
- Pruning shears
- Stakes and ties (optional)
- Mulch
- An adult to help

WHEN TO PLANT

Where winters are not severe: fall
Where winters are severe: as early in spring as you can dig

Pick a good spot for your tree
An ideal spot for a dwarf fruit tree has good air circulation, to reduce the chances of diseases such as mildew, and protection from strong winds. The soil should be slightly acid (a pH of 5.5 to 6.5) and—most important—well drained.

In the north, the spot should also have good "air drainage," to protect your tree from early frost. Avoid a "pocket" at the foot of a hill into which heavy, cold air will sink. A slight slope is usually less susceptible to frost.

Dig a big hole —ahead of time
You need a giant-sized hole to plant even a dwarf tree. The best way to do this is to prepare the tree hole *several months* before planting time. With a spade or shovel, start digging! Ask an adult to help. The poorer the soil, the larger your hole should be. Three feet by 3 feet by 2 feet deep isn't too big. Generally, make it at least twice as wide and half again as deep as the root ball.

Make a compost pit in the hole
Make in-place compost to provide humusy soil in which tree roots can grow easily. Layer the best soil from the hole with organic material—manure, chopped leaves, grass clippings, kitchen refuse, weeds, even zucchini that grew too large to eat. It's like making a

VARIATIONS

Give any kind of tree as a gift to mark a special occasion. The rules for planting are the same. Tree planting is a good project for a class or group of children.

BOUNTY
▲ **Apples are the ripened ovaries of flowers.**

BLOSSOMS
▶ **In spring, delicate white blossoms bedeck Karyn's dwarf apple tree.**

WHAT ARE LEAVES FOR?

Leaves are the food factories for plants. In the leaves is a magical substance called chlorophyll, which gives them their green color. It allows leaves to use energy from sunlight and the raw materials of water, minerals, and carbon dioxide to make the food the plant needs for growth. Food-making in plants has a fifty-dollar name: PHOTOSYNTHESIS.

Plants also "breathe" through tiny holes in the undersides of leaves.

TREE PLANTING

▶ **A) Make the hole at least twice as wide and half again as deep as the root ball.**

B) Layer it with the raw materials for compost a few months before planting time.

C) Put a mound of rich soil in the bottom of the hole.

D) Spread tree roots over the mound of soil. Fill the hole, leaving a watering trough. Keep the union 2 to 3 inches above soil level.

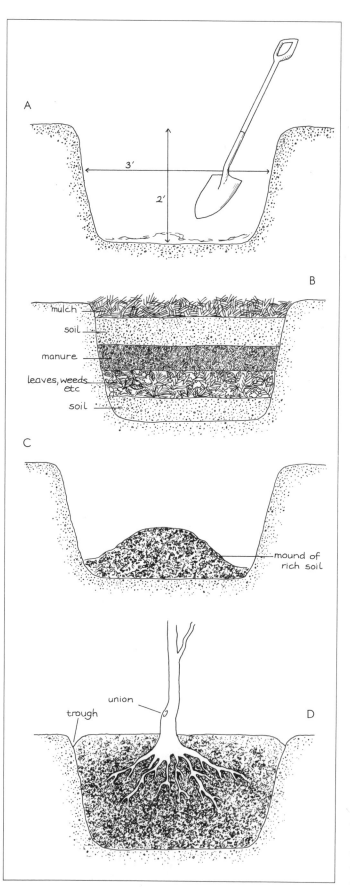

cake, with a layer of soil, a layer of organic material such as hay, weeds, or leaves, and a layer of high-nitrogen material such as manure or dried blood (see p. 33). The decomposition will be fastest if the organic matter is in small pieces. Ask a grownup to run a rotary lawnmower through the compost material before you make your layer cake. Finish the cake with a layer of soil and mulch thickly with hay, straw, or shredded bark.

It's important to do all this a few months ahead of planting so that everything is decomposed beforehand. Otherwise, your young tree will be robbed of nitrogen, which is used in the process of decomposition.

What to plant?
In the north, choose a dwarf apple or pear tree. Apple blossoms are deliciously fragrant in spring. In warmer climates, try a dwarf peach. Apricots, quinces, plums, and cherries also come in dwarf form. In places where it is warm in winter, plant a dwarf citrus. Ask your county agent to suggest a variety that does well in your climate.

Order bare-rooted stock from a mail-order nursery, or buy trees in cans of soil from your local nursery. Buy only rootstock named by variety, at least two years old.

How to plant
If you've made your hole ahead of time, it will be easy as pie to remove the loose soil and pile it on a tarp.

If you haven't dug ahead of planting time, fill the excavated hole one-third full with compost, peat moss, and/or well-rotted manure. Add an equal amount of good soil and mix.

Fill the hole with enough of the rich mixed soil so that the bulge in the trunk (called the union), which shows where the rootstock and the scion (top part) were grafted, will be 2 to 3 inches ABOVE soil level after the tree is planted. Make a mound of this rich soil.

Prune the roots
Keep roots of a bare-root tree wet until planting. Use sharp pruning shears to cut off any broken or dried-out roots, or any that are too long to fit in the hole.

Set the tree
Place the tree on the mound of rich soil at the bottom of the hole. Check the level as described above. Add rich soil around and over the roots, holding the tree erect as you fill. The least rich soil can go on top. Do not hill up the soil around the trunk. Make a ring-shaped trough around the edge of the hole that is about 4 inches deeper than ground level. Firm the soil around the roots by stepping on it.

DO NOT ADD COMMERCIAL FERTILIZER AT PLANTING TIME! You may burn tender roots and stimulate too much top growth before roots are established. The rich soil around the roots will slowly feed the young tree.

No air pockets, please! Settle the soil around the roots. Water deeply with a gentle trickle until the soil around the edge of the hole is also wet. Wait a half hour and soak again.

Prune
Ask a grownup to cut back the top of the tree. Shorten branches just above a healthy, outward-facing bud, cutting down from the bud at a 45° angle. Cut out any broken or crossing branches. That will give the roots a chance to grow without too much top growth to support.

Stake the tree if you wish.

Care for your tree
■ WATER. Dwarf fruit trees have a shallow root system. Whenever your garden needs extra water, give some to your tree. Water slowly and deeply. The basin around your tree should help water get to the roots.

■ MULCH. Keep moisture in and the soil cool with a thick layer of shredded bark, straw, grass clippings, chopped-up leaves, compost, or manure. Never put the mulch next to the trunk. Keep it a few inches away, to keep from encouraging mice and fungus.

■ FERTILIZE. Sprinkle ¼ pound of fertilizer out to the drip line (an imaginary line from the outermost branches to the ground) of the tree in early spring, starting the year after planting. Keep the fertilizer a few inches away from the trunk. When the tree is five years old, increase the

amount to ½ or ¾ pound.

■ THIN FRUIT. When the fruit is marble-sized, pick off extras, so that apples, pears, peaches, and nectarines are 6 inches apart. Plums and apricots should be 3 inches apart. Cherries and quinces don't need thinning. This lets the tree's energy go into making bigger, better fruit, and keeps limbs from breaking from too heavy a load.

■ PRUNE. Dwarf trees need less pruning than standard-sized trees. In winter, ask a grownup to remove dead, diseased, broken, or crossing branches, and to thin out branches so the inside of the tree is light and airy. Make sure tools are sharp.

■ PROTECT TRUNK FROM RODENTS. In fall, sink a cylinder of hardware cloth into the ground around the trunk, to keep mice and voles from nibbling on the bark.

FRUIT

▲ **By autumn, an apple has developed from a spring blossom.**

▼ **Karyn and her mom turn the handle to begin pressing juice from the pomace.**

MAKE APPLE CIDER

Grind or grate apples and press out the juice, for a tasty, healthful drink.

Make the pomace
Wash apples thoroughly, then grate or grind them. Use a hand grater, a meat grinder, or, with adult help, an electric food processor with a grating attachment. The chopped-up apple pulp is called "pomace."

Press the cider
Load the grated apples into the mill. You may put the pomace in a press bag, but this is not necessary for all small home presses.

Put the cover in place, set a stainless or enameled pot or basin under the press to catch the juice, and screw down the handle until it presses firmly on the pomace. Continue to tighten it gradually over a period of four or five hours, until the cider is extracted.

Enjoy!
You may want to strain the cider or pour it through a layer of cheesecloth or nylon netting before you drink it. Then enjoy the hearty taste of fall. Mmm, good!

Refrigerate any unused cider. You can freeze it, too. Just leave a little space in the container for expansion during freezing.

◄ **Ground-up apples, called pomace, are ready for pressing.**

DRYING

▼ **Apple rings are strung for drying.**

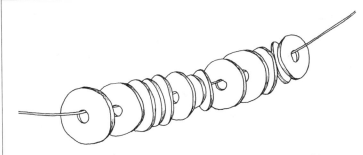

MAKE DRIED APPLE SLICES

Prepare the apples
Wash and dry the apples. Ask a grownup to help you remove the cores. Slice the apples into rings about ¼ inch thick.

Dry the apples
Thread the apple slices on a string and hang in a dry and airy place. Cover the drying apples with cheesecloth to protect them from dirt.

Eat!
When the apple slices are dry, pack them into a container and use for snacks. Hang some from your Christmas tree. Or cook them in a little water with cinnamon, honey, nuts, and raisins for a delicious winter dessert.

YOU NEED
- Ripe, firm apples
- An apple corer
- A knife and cutting board
- A string
- Cheesecloth

TIME OF YEAR
Fall

ENJOYING

▲ **Freshly pressed apple cider is deee-licious!**

YOU NEED
- Apples
- A hand grater, meat grinder, or food processor
- A small, hand cider press
- A nylon press bag (optional)
- A bowl and ladle
- Cheesecloth, nylon net filter, or strainer
- A stainless-steel or enameled container for the cider
- Glasses

TIME OF YEAR
Fall

HOMEWARD BOUND

▼ **Danny and his dog Kerry haul a harvested Christmas tree to the house.**

START A CHRISTMAS TREE FARM

Photo by Linda Tilgner

Take four boys, ages thirteen, twelve, ten, and eight. Add a heavy schedule of spring, summer, and fall soccer, vacations, play with friends, and plain ol' horsing around. Plug in a need for revenue for future education. What do you come up with for a gardening project? A Christmas tree farm—requiring a concerted group effort to plant new trees and fertilize established ones in early spring, a shearing marathon in early summer, a cooperative adult willing to mow around the trees twice a year, and camaraderie in December each time a customer comes to have one cut.

Their dad admits planting Christmas trees would be a lot faster and neater to do by himself. (That makes it about the same as any project shared with children!) "We laid out the string so carefully and it got all wrapped around Tim's leg," he told me. "Make sure the boys show you that crooked row."

Pat, Dan, Tim, and Mike White started their tree farm on a half acre of gently sloping land above their pond in 1981, when Pat, the oldest, was only eight. Not only have they worked together to plant and care for the trees, but they have kept records of purchases, dates of planting, fertilizing, shearing, and cutting, and have written letters to order their trees.

They planted 400 trees in 1981. They've added 30 to 100 new trees each year. Recently, they've ordered new ones primarily to replace those that have died or have been cut.

Christmas trees can be grown wherever trees grow—in every part of the United States except arid areas, such as the deserts of the Southwest or the plains of the Midwest.

A Christmas tree farm is a perfect project for a large family or an organized group of children—a 4-H club, a youth garden club, or scouts. Plant a small plantation, or follow the guidelines to plant a grove with a tree for each family member. Even if you don't grow your own, visit a commercial Christmas tree plantation to choose and cut your own tree for the holidays.

Choose the site
A clear pasture or a recently used hayfield is an ideal site for a Christmas tree farm. If woody plants are already growing on the site you want to use, site preparation will be needed. See your county forester or county agent before you plant. It's a lot easier to get your land in shape before you plant than after!

Order the tree seedlings
During the winter, call your county forester, county extension agent, or Soil Conservation Service representative, to ask what varieties are recommended for your locality, and to find out about the availability of Christmas tree seedlings in

YOU NEED

- Open land (Christmas trees need sunshine!)
- String and stakes
- Christmas tree seedlings
- A bucket of water
- A tree-planting bar (sold through forestry supply and garden catalogs)
- A knife or clippers
- A fertilizer tablet for each seedling (10-gram, 20-10-5)
- Simazine or mulch
- A record book
- A camera (to record growth of trees and children)
- Granulated fertilizer
- Hedge clippers

WHEN TO PLANT

Early spring (however, trees must be ordered well ahead of planting time)

your state. Here in Vermont, the minimum order from the state nursery is 200, but our local SCS agent sometimes buys some to sell in small quantities to homeowners.

If small quantities are not available, ask for the name of a nearby commercial grower who buys a lot of seedlings each year. Call to find out if she will order some extras for you. That's how the White boys have obtained seedlings of balsam fir, Frasier fir, Douglas fir, Black Hills spruce, Scotch pine, eastern white pine, and southwestern white pine.

Some trees cost 12 cents apiece, some 50 cents. Jim White says, "Never try to save money on planting stock. Buy the best. If you want to cut corners, plant fewer trees."

How many?
On an acre of open land, you can plant 1,200 seedlings with 6-foot by 6-foot spacing. Use that ratio in figuring how many trees to order. Order several varieties, and plant only part of the land each year.

Keep roots wet
Keep seedlings in a bucket of water until they go into the ground. Never let the roots dry out!

Lay out the rows
With stakes and string, lay out rows 6 feet apart. Mark tree planting locations with stakes 6 feet apart in each row.

Plant the trees
Planting is best done as a

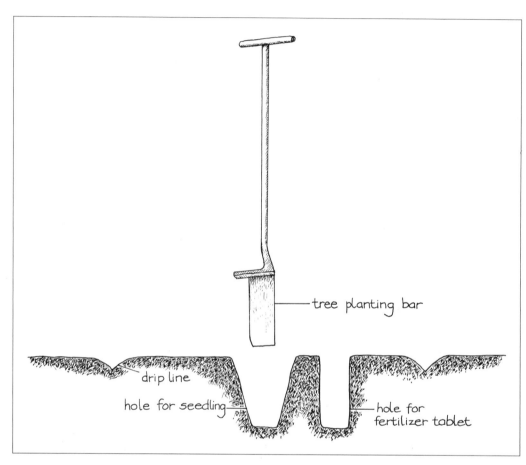

tree planting bar

drip line

hole for seedling

hole for fertilizer tablet

USING PLANTING BAR

▲ **Rock the planting bar back and forth to open one hole for the seedling, another for the fertilizer tablet, and insert it a third time to close up the first two holes.**

PLANTING

▶ **Tim inserts the seedling into the hole Patrick has made with the tree planting bar.**

team effort, as soon as possible after seedlings arrive.

■ JOB #1: PRUNE THE ROOTS. Take a seedling out of the bucket. Cut off long or broken roots with a sharp knife or clippers.

■ JOB #2: MAN THE TREE-PLANTING BAR. Three holes are needed for each tree: to plant the tree, to insert the fertilizer tablet, and to close the hole. Insert the bar into the ground. Push with your foot until the crosspiece hits the ground. Rock the bar back and forth to open a hole for the seedling.

■ JOB #3: INSERT THE SEED-

LING. Put the seedling into the hole so that it is at the same level it grew in the nursery.

■ JOB #4: ADD THE FERTIL-IZER TABLET. Make a second hole with the tree-planting bar 2 inches away from the seedling. Drop a fertilizer tablet into the hole. This compressed plant food will slowly release nutrients to the young seedling for two years.

■ JOB #5: CLOSE THE HOLES. With the planting bar, make a third hole next to the seedling. Close the bottom of the seedling's hole first, by

FERTILIZER TABLET

▲ **Mike buries one fertilizer tablet next to each seedling at planting time.**

WHY DO PLANTS NEED WATER?

Most plants are ninety percent water. Water is one of the raw materials plants use, along with minerals from the soil and carbon dioxide from the air, to manufacture their own food. Plants are really food-making factories!

pulling back on the bar. Then push it forward to close the top of the hole. Stamp the ground with your foot to firm the soil even more.

■ JOB #6: TUG ON THE TREE. Pull on the tree to make sure it is snugly set in the ground. You don't want a big air pocket down there!

Control weeds

Jim White says, "There are only three problems in trying to grow high-quality trees: weeds, weeds, and weeds." You must control weed growth around the trees. Otherwise, grasses will grow higher than the tree, choking it out, shutting off sunshine, and using up all the fertilizer you buried to help the tree grow. If you fertilize without controlling weeds, you're actually setting back the tree, because you're giving food to the "competition," helping already established grasses grow mammoth.

The easiest way to control weeds is to apply granular simazine to the area around each tree. This selective chemical kills annual grasses but not broadleaf or woody plants. One application will last for a couple of years. Ask a grownup to apply it carefully, according to manufacturer's directions.

If you prefer, mulch around each seedling until it is waist high.

Mow twice a year

Here's when you need a friendly grownup, to mow between and around trees, once in late June and again in early August. The person

who mows will thank you for controlling the weeds. If you hadn't, he wouldn't be able to spot the seedlings among the tall grasses and would probably mow most of them down!

Keep records

Write down dates and expenses (or income) for all the important things you do: when you order; what you order; when you plant, fertilize, mow, shear, sell, etc.

What next?

Most of your trees should grow and prosper, but some of them will die. Tree farmers usually lose about ten percent of their trees.

When trees are waist high, you need to fertilize and shear.

Fertilize established trees

Your trees could live without it, but fertilizer makes them a darker, healthier green and helps them produce more buds.

Apply 10-10-10 granulated fertilizer by holding it at waist height and sprinkling it all over and around the tree out to the drip line, but not close to the stem. Then knock it off the tree so it falls to the ground. Danny White explains that this method ensures that "it doesn't get in a big pile in one spot and just a little bit in another."

How much? Trees knee height to waist height get two 4-ounce cups; waist height to shoulder height get three 4-ounce cups; and those above shoulder height get four 4-ounce cups.

Shear established trees
Start shearing when trees are waist high. This shaping slows down top growth, and makes trees produce more lateral growth, so they look full and bushy.

Clip the top leader first. Limit its growth to 14 inches. (If it's shorter, you don't need to prune it.) With pruning shears, cut ¼ inch above a large bud, on a 45° angle

HOW OLD?

Do you know how to tell the age of a Christmas tree? Start at the ground and count the "whorls" (the place where a bunch of branches grow out of the trunk) as you go up the trunk. The space between each whorl is one year's growth.

FEEDING

▲ **Danny and Tim feed established trees in early spring by sprinkling granular fertilizer on the branches, then shake the branches to sift the granules evenly over the soil.**

WHY DO WE PRUNE TREES AND SHRUBS?

When we plant a tree or shrub, we prune, or cut back, the top growth so the roots won't have more work than they can handle in gathering water and minerals for too many leaves. That gives the root system a chance to grow strong and healthy.

Gardeners prune fruit trees regularly, to help them produce bigger and better fruit. Sometimes they train trees or shrubs to grow in a special shape.

CUTTING

▲ **Mike watches brother Danny cut a tree.**

TRIMMING

◄ **Jim White, county forester, shows son Danny how to trim the leader at a 45° angle, ¼ inch above a large bud.**

slanting down away from the bud.

Next, taper the shape of the tree to get good form. A spruce or fir tree should have a width at the bottom two-thirds that of the height. A 6-foot-high tree, for instance, should be 4 feet wide at the bottom. Pines are generally wider, with a bottom width three-fourths of the tree's height.

Draw an imaginary line from the clipped leader to the ground, like an upside-down ice cream cone. With hedge clippers, shear off anything that sticks out beyond that imaginary line.

CAUTION! Shearing is an important job. A child should never do it without adult help and guidance. Otherwise, you may be saying,

"Whoops! There goes five years' work."

Cut the trees

When a tree is about 7 feet high, it is ready to cut as a Christmas tree. Not all trees planted at the same time will be ready for sale at the same time. In the north, most spruce and fir will be the right size when they've been growing in the field for about nine years, but some will be big enough after seven years, and others will need eleven years of field growth. Pines are ready a little sooner; they peak at seven or eight years.

In the south, where different species prosper, trees mature much more quickly. It takes only three or four years to grow a market-size tree. You must shear three times a year, however.

"This year we gave away ten trees and sold one. It's the boys' way of saying 'thank you' to people who have been good to them. Every time someone came to cut a tree it turned into a party." (Cathy White, mom)

MAPLE SUGARING, THE FIFTH SEASON

Photo by Linda Tilgner

BOILING DOWN

▲ **"This looks and smells more and more like maple syrup!" exclaim Will, Greg, and Jamie.**

Spring, summer, fall, winter, and then comes a softening. Warming sun brings daytime temperatures above freezing; they snap back to crackling cold at night. Maple sap begins to flow. The fifth season has begun.

Wherever sugar maples thrive, buckets and tubing decorate the woods and roadsides, collecting the slightly sweet sap. Clouds of steam rise from sugar houses. To those who participate, as makers or observers, this is a special time of year.

"Sugaring always seemed to help us bring spring about earlier," says Sheri Crittendon. "You want to get out into the woods. You can *feel* spring coming. It's different from the silence of winter. Everything comes alive and you can see it first-hand. Birds sing. Icicles drip. The first pussywillows bloom. I feel like a caged animal now that we no longer sugar."

Share with a child this wondrous time in some way: visit a sugar house, boil a gallon of maple sap at home, start your own small family sugaring operation, or have a sugar-on-snow party.

VISIT A SUGAR HOUSE, THEN BOIL A GALLON OF SAP INDOORS

Most sugarmakers welcome visitors while they spend long hours in front of the evaporator. A sugarmaker will show you the arch, where the fire roars; the evaporator, with its many rooms; the special instruments for testing the sap; the spigot for drawing off finished syrup; and the filters for straining out impurities. You may even be given a taste of fresh, warm syrup.

Perhaps you can talk the sugarmaker into selling you a gallon of sap to boil down at home. It's the only graphic way to show a child how much sap it takes to get a tiny bit of maple syrup. It's also a wonderful demonstration of evaporation and condensation.

Boil the sap
Keep the sap refrigerated until you are ready to boil. It's best to use it right away. Taste it. It's really a lot like water. Can you detect a slight sweetness?

Pour the sap into the kettle and place on high heat. Boil, boil, boil! If the sap threatens to boil over the top of the kettle, add a tiny piece of butter to make the foam subside. It will take hours for most of the water to evaporate. Watch the steam condense on your windowpanes!

YOU NEED

- A gallon of sap
- A strainer
- A large kettle
- Butter
- A small pot
- A large spoon
- A stove

TIME OF YEAR

Late February and March, when maple sap flows

"Finish" in a small pot
When the sap has reduced to about a cupful and begins to look tan, pour it into a small pot to finish the evaporation. This goes quickly, and you might burn the syrup if you keep it in the large kettle. Test it by letting it drip from a spoon. When two drops come together and fall in a "sheet," it is syrup. From a gallon of sap, expect to get ⅓ to ½ cup of syrup, a 30- or 40-to-one ratio, depending on the sugar content of the sap. Taste. Mmmm!

▼ Geoff taps a sugar maple, angling the bit slightly uphill so the sap will run into the bucket.

Photo by Linda Tilgner

START A SMALL-SCALE SUGARING OPERATION

Geoffrey, Katharine, and Peter Wittreich work with their parents to tap a few sugar maples near their house. Their father George says it's "an exercise in the rites of spring. The object is not to be efficient, but to relax as much as you can."

Try it!
Scrub-a-dub
Wash and rinse the buckets, spouts, trash can, and evaporating pan, and let them air dry.

Tap the trees
A tree must be 10 inches in diameter before it can be tapped. Trees with a diameter of 10 to 14 inches may get one tap; from 15 to 19 inches can take two taps; from 20 to 24 inches, three taps; and

YOU NEED

- Some sugar maple trees, at least 10 inches in diameter
- A brace and a 7/16-inch wood bit
- A hammer
- Spouts and hooks
- Covered containers to hang on the spouts (sugaring buckets are best, but some people use plastic gallon jugs or gallon cans with makeshift covers)
- A clean 20-gallon trash can
- Plastic garbage bags to line the trash can
- A garden cart
- A place to build a fire and firewood (slab wood is often used) or a 2-burner hot plate
- A large, shallow pan in which to boil the sap (special evaporating pans are available from suppliers)
- A large scoop or spoon
- A candy thermometer or hydrometer (optional)
- A strainer
- Filters
- Cans or canning jars in which to store syrup

TIME OF YEAR

Late February and early March, when days are above freezing and nights are below freezing

those over 25 inches, four taps.

With the brace and bit, drill a hole for each spout, angling the bit slightly upward, so the sap will run down into the pail. Drill through the bark into the outer sapwood, just under the cambium, about 2 to 3 inches. Clear the shavings from the hole.

Tap in a spout with the hammer. Hang a bucket on the hook. Cover the bucket. When the sap flows you will hear a plink, plink, plink— the gentle music of the trees.

Gather the sap
Place the plastic liner inside the trash can. Put the trash can in the garden cart. Pour sap from the buckets into the trash can. Collect daily when sap is running.

Boil, boil, boil
Get a hot fire going. Use an outdoor cinder-block fireplace with a metal grate on which to place a large kettle or pan for boiling. (The Wittreichs started that way. Then they purchased a small evaporating rig and an arch made from half a metal drum.) On a smaller scale, boil on an electric hot plate in the garage. In any case, don't try this in the house. The steam will take the wallpaper off the walls.

Strain the sap before adding it to the evaporator. Boil until the syrup is ready—when it sheets from a

Photo by Linda Tilgner

HOW MUCH?

▲ **Peter peeks at the dripping maple sap before he empties the bucket.**

sugar maple leaf

spoon, or when it reaches 7°F above the boiling point of water (which changes daily according to the barometric pressure; stick the candy thermometer in boiling water to calibrate it before you begin). It usually takes several hours. You may find it easier to "finish" the syrup—do the last bit of boiling—in the kitchen, in a smaller pot.

Filter and can
Pour the hot syrup through a filter. Keep it above 180°F

Photo by Linda Tilgner

GATHERING

▲ **"Wow, that's a lot of sap!" David, Sarah, and Leslie inspect the sap in the metal drum used as a gathering tank.**

STRAINING

◄ **Katharine strains the sap as she adds it to the evaporator.**

Photo by Linda Tilgner

and pour it into maple syrup cans. Cover immediately, and tilt the can so that the hot syrup touches the inside of the lid to sterilize it.

Or pour the hot syrup into mason jars and process in a boiling water bath for 5 minutes.

Store in a cool place. (You can also freeze maple syrup.)

If mold appears on the surface, don't worry. It's harmless. Reboil and skim. Use syrup on pancakes and ice cream, or give as gifts.

Photo by Linda Tilgner

BOILING

▲ **Geoff replenishes the wood supply that fuels the evaporator. Steam rises from the bubbling sap.**

HAVE A SUGAR-ON-SNOW PARTY

This is a traditional, festive celebration at the end of sugaring season. Keep some snow in the freezer until you need it. If you don't live in snow country, use a child's Sno-Cone maker or an ice-crushing attachment on your blender to make "artificial snow."

Thicken the syrup
Hang the candy thermometer on the pot. Pour in the syrup and boil until it reaches 238°F and/or forms a soft ball

YOU NEED

- A pint or quart of maple syrup
- A large pot
- A candy thermometer
- A large spoon
- A glass of ice-cold water
- Dishes of snow
- Forks or popsicle sticks
- Sour pickles
- Donuts
- Apple cider
- People for a party

TIME OF YEAR

March

when you drop it into ice-cold water.

Sugar-on-snow
Drizzle the thickened syrup on each person's dish of snow. It will become waxy and taffy-like. Lift and twist strings of it with the fork or popsicle stick. Eat. Mmm, sweet!

Antidotes
Eat a sour pickle to take away the sweetness of the maple taffy. Take a bite of donut to take away the sourness of the pickle. Sip apple cider to quench your thirst. Then start all over again. Have fun!

GROW A TREE INDOORS

A city child can plant seeds to grow a tree from scratch. Place it in a sunny indoor spot in winter, and let it summer on a balcony, terrace, or fire escape. Country kids can do this, too!

YOU NEED

- An avocado
- Toothpicks
- A jar or glass of water
- Lots of patience
- A flower pot
- Crockery or pebbles
- Planting mix or potting soil

TIME OF YEAR

Any time

TOOTHPICKS

▶ **Sean watches Erin poke toothpicks into the avocado pit.**

GROW AN AVOCADO TREE

Eat the fruit and plant the pit!

Find the seed
Eat the avocado. It's terrific in a tossed salad or as a Mexican dip called guacamole. Inside is a *huge* seed.

Start the seed
Let the pit dry for a day or two. Peel off the brown skin. Insert three toothpicks so you can suspend it in the jar of water with the base of the pit in the water. The pointed end is the top.

CORRECT DEPTH

▲ **Suspend the avocado pit so that its base is in water.**

Wait, wait, wait

Put the jar in a warm spot away from sun until roots form. Keep adding warm water to the jar to keep the bottom third of the pit in water. It may take several weeks for anything to happen. (Sometimes a pit just won't sprout!)

Roots!

When you see roots, shout "hooray!" and move the jar to a sunny place. When a stem pushes up, wait until it gets 3 or 4 inches high.

Soil, at last

Place some crockery or pebbles in the bottom of the flower pot, hold the pit in place, and fill the pot with moistened planting mix or potting soil. Let about a half-inch of the top of the pit stick out of the soil. Water well.

What next?

Keep the plant in a sunny spot. When leaves begin to form, snip off the tip of the stem to encourage side branching. Enjoy your beautiful avocado tree!

DOES IT MATTER IF YOU PLANT A SEED UPSIDE-DOWN?

Try it! The roots of plants are "programmed" to grow down, the stems to grow up. See what happens if you plant a seed upside-down.

GROW A CITRUS TREE

Start a windowsill orchard.

Soak the seeds

Soak the seeds in water for a day or two to hasten germination.

Plant the seeds

Place crockery or pebbles in the bottom of small flower pots. Fill with moistened planting mix or potting soil. Plant three seeds in each pot, about ½ inch deep. Water well.

Label the pots

Write the name of the fruit and the date of planting on a label or tongue depressor and stick it into the soil.

Watch and wait

In a few weeks, tiny seedlings will sprout. Snip off all but one, or transplant each to its own pot. Watch them grow into bushy, shiny-leaved, small trees. Let them spend summers outdoors.

Will they fruit?

Alas, these trees will not bear fruit for at least five years. If you're anxious to harvest fruit, buy a dwarf fruit tree, such as a Meyer lemon or a Calamondin orange. See dwarf fruit tree (p. 118) and container growing (p. 106).

YOU NEED

- Grapefruit, orange, or lemon seeds
- A glass of water
- Small flower pots
- Crockery or pebbles
- Planting mix
- Plastic labels or tongue depressors
- A watering can

TIME OF YEAR

Any time

CITRUS

▲ **Grapefruit, orange, and lemon seeds produce glossy-leaved seedlings.**

FINALLY!

◄ **After a long wait, Erin is rewarded when her avocado tree produces stems and leaves.**

CHAPTER 9

LET'S DISCOVER! GARDEN HELPERS

GATHERING

▲ **A honeybee forages for nectar and pollen inside a rose.**

BEEHIVE

▶ **This hive is ready for winter with a mouse guard across the entrance to keep mice from making a home inside.**

Children love things that are ALIVE! They'll be the first to find the praying mantis, the spider in its web, the toad, the turtle, or the garter snake. They're fascinated by all manner of creepy, crawly things. Capitalize on this natural curiosity by introducing children to the partnership between plants and beneficial creatures. Teach them to tell helpful creatures from destructive ones. Through this they will begin to understand the ideas of balance, predator and prey, and interconnectedness in the natural world, of which the garden is a part.

Encourage the population of beneficial creatures in the garden. Plant to attract bees, butterflies, and birds. Set a bird bath or a toad house in the garden. Clap when you see ladybugs devouring aphids, or a snake slithering between the beans.

DISCOVER POLLINATORS: BEES

Introduce a child to bees, garden helpers supreme. Without bees as pollinators, we'd be without much of our food and many of our flowers.

Busy as a bee is no joke. They are busy indeed! Help a child to learn about the queen bee, one to a hive, non-stop layer of thousands of eggs; about the male drones, a hundred to a hive, who have a lazy life until they mate and die, or are kicked out of the hive by females when cold sets in; about the female workers, 20,000 or more to a hive, who act as nursemaids, chambermaids, air conditioners, evaporators, nectar and pollen gatherers, soldiers, and construction engineers.

Although young children cannot themselves be beekeepers, they might enjoy visiting one who will don the special gear worn in caring for bees. Ask her to explain how the smoker is used to drowse bees when checking the hives, and to show you the frames that hold the delicate yet sturdy waxen honeycomb, its cells filled with honey, pollen, or bees in various stages of development.

The O'Brien family has five hives. Erin talks about the queen. "Sometimes Daddy has to get a new queen, if the queen is all worn out from laying eggs and telling the workers what to do."

Erin and her brother Justin help with the twice-a-year honey harvest. Their parents cut the caps off the combs. The children spin out the honey in the extractor, and thereby learn about centrifugal force.

Bees are attracted primarily to color, and secondarily to scent. Yellow is their favorite color, followed by blues and purples. Bees see color differently than you do—a white flower may appear in many colors of purple to a bee. And bees are attracted to sweet smells—if you use perfume or scented shampoo, they might harass you.

To entice bees to your garden, plant clumps of these in sunny spots:

Anthemis, sundrops, rudbeckia, thermopsis, lemon balm, borage, sage, thyme, lavender, sweet alyssum, nasturtium, poppy, catnip, daisy, globe thistle, beebalm, mignonette, meadowsweet, Jacob's ladder, delphinium, forget-me-not, campanula, love-in-a-mist, clovers, chamomile, flax, salvia.

HOW DO BEES HELP GARDENERS?

In their travels from flower to flower to gather nectar, bees act as nature's pollinators. Without bees (and butterflies, some insects, and hummingbirds), we would not have apples, peaches, and many other kinds of fruit!

DISCOVER BIRDS

Many birds are bug-gobblers, eating enormous quantities of insects each day. For lunch, a scarlet tanager can gobble 1,000 gypsy moth caterpillars, a flicker 3,000 ants, or a yellow-billed cuckoo 250 tent caterpillars. Birds eat constantly, and most of them are friends to your garden.

Help your child play detective. The shape of a bird's beak is a clue to its diet. Insect eaters have straight, narrow bills. Seed eaters have heavy, thick bills. Soon, you and the child will come to know some of the birds as friends, and recognize the joyful whistle of a cardinal or the happy chatter of a chickadee.

Tiniest of all is the hummingbird. My family often watched in amazement as a male ruby-throat hovered over the red monarda, wings a blur, thrusting his needle-like bill in and out of the trumpet-shaped petals. We and our children could share a miracle because of a flower we'd planted in our garden.

You can plant to attract birds in general, or hummingbirds in particular.

Birds like variety—tall trees, thick shrubs, and low vines. Some people worry that birds will steal their garden berries, but they'd rather eat tart, wild fruit if it's there.

PLANT FOR THE BIRDS

- TREES. Sassafras, shadbush, larch, tupelo, Canadian hemlock, holly, red cedar, mountain ash, flowering dogwood, chokecherry, pin cherry, crabapple, hawthorn, tulip tree, hackberry, buckthorn, mulberry, poplar, birch, oak, pine, spruce.
- SHRUBS. Staghorn sumac, Russian olive, autumn olive, bush honeysuckle, American cranberry, firethorn, red osier and silky dogwood, bayberry, Japanese barberry, cotoneaster, inkberry, juniper, rugosa and multiflora rose, elderberry, Japanese yew, viburnum.
- VINES. Virginia creeper, wild grapes, bittersweet.
- HUMMINGBIRDS are drawn to red and orange trumpet-shaped flowers: red beebalm (*Monarda didyma*), red salvia, snapdragon, balloon flower, daylily, coral bells, columbine, false dragonhead, globe thistle, nicotiana, lily, lupine, lilac, penstemon, phlox, hollyhocks, trumpet vine, Japanese flowering quince, weigela.

PUT A BIRD BATH IN THE GARDEN

You don't need to buy a fancy bird bath. You can concoct a homemade one in a few minutes.

YOU NEED

- A sturdy log, 10 to 18 inches high
- A large terra-cotta saucer (the kind made for placing under flower pots)
- Water

TIME OF YEAR

Spring through fall

Assemble the bird bath
Make sure the ends of the log are cut square, so it is steady when upright. Set it on end in the lawn or near the flower garden. Keep it away from overhanging branches or shrubs from which cats might pounce! Put the terra-cotta saucer on top of the log and fill it with water.

Keep it clean
Refill the water daily and scrub the saucer once a week. See who comes to bathe!

DEPENDENT

▲ Once birds start coming to a feeder, it must be kept full all winter, especially during snowstorms and cold weather.

NESTING BOXES

SPECIES	FLOOR	HEIGHT	ENTRANCE ABOVE FLOOR	DIAMETER OF ENTRANCE	HEIGHT ABOVE GROUND
Bluebird	4 x 4"	8-12"	6-10"	1½"	3-6'
Chickadee	4 x 4	9	7	1⅛	4-15
Great Crested Flycatcher	6 x 6	8-10	6-8	1¾	8-20
Nuthatch	4 x 4	9	7	1⅜	5-15
Phoebe	6 x 6	6			8-12
Robin	6 x 8	8			6-15
Barn Swallow	6 x 6	6			8-12
Purple Martin	6 x 6	6	1	2¼	10-20
Tree Swallow	5 x 5	6-8	4-6	1½	4-15
Titmouse	4 x 4	9	7	1¼	5-15
Downy Woodpecker	4 x 4	9	7	1¼	5-15
Flicker	7 x 7	16-18	14-16	2½	6-30
Hairy Woodpecker	6 x 6	12-15	9-12	1⅝	12-20
Red-headed Woodpecker	6 x 6	12	9	2	10-20
Bewick's Wren	4 x 4	6-8	4-6	1¼	5-10
Carolina Wren	4 x 4	6-8	4-6	1½	5-10
House Wren	4 x 4	6-8	4-6	1-1¼	4-10

BUILD A BIRD HOUSE

Here's a joint project for a child and an adult who like to work with wood.

Cut, drill, and sand
Cut the wood according to the plan. Drill two drainage holes in the bottom.

Drill an entry hole in the front. The size of the hole is very important, so that only the bird, and not its enemies, can get in. Consult the chart, and pick the correct diameter for the kind of bird you want to attract.

Drill a smaller hole for the dowel. Sand all rough edges.

Assemble
Nail together the sides, back, front, and bottom. Attach the back to the mounting board. Set the roof in place and drill holes for hinges. Screw in place. Stain a natural wood color.

Install
See chart for how high to hang the house. Birds will be safer from predators if you put in on a post or pole, rather than on a tree, in a place protected from wind and in partial sun.

YOU NEED

- A piece of wood 1 inch by 4 inches by 41 inches
- A piece of wood 1 inch by 8 inches by 8½ inches
- A piece of wood 1 inch by 4 inches by 18 inches
- A 2-inch-long dowel
- 2 hinges
- Screws for the hinges
- Nails
- Saw, hammer, screwdriver, drill and bits
- Sandpaper

TIME OF YEAR

Make it in winter; put it up in spring

MAKE A CHRISTMAS TREE FOR THE BIRDS

After you finish with your Christmas tree, stake it outside as a feeding station.

DECORATE IT WITH

- Pine cones stuffed with peanut butter
- Strings of cranberry, popcorn, and dried fruit
- Small mesh bags of suet
- Nosegays of wheat or other grains
- Half rinds of oranges filled with bird seed
- Small ears of corn
- Small dried heads of sunflowers

About feeding the birds
Once you begin feeding the birds, they will depend on you for food. Don't let them down. Stock a few feeders, so birds can move to another if frightened by a predator. Put feeders near shrubs or trees, so birds can perch there to check out the situation before they feed.

You can rig a simple feeder from a half-gallon milk carton or a gallon plastic jug. Or drill holes in a small log. Stuff with peanut butter or suet and hang up.

If you are very patient, you may be able to coax a chickadee to take a sunflower seed right from your

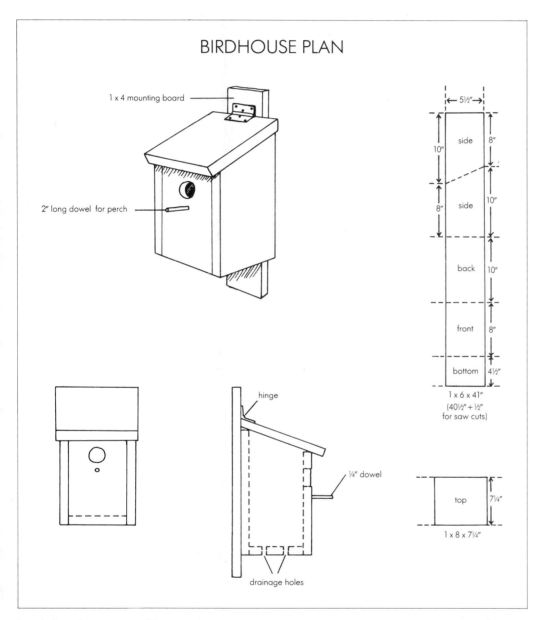

BIRDHOUSE PLAN

1 x 4 mounting board

2" long dowel for perch

5½"

side — 8"

10"

side — 10"

8"

back — 10"

front — 8"

bottom — 4½"

1 x 6 x 41"
(40½" + ½"
for saw cuts)

hinge

¼" dowel

top — 7¼"

1 x 8 x 7¼"

drainage holes

▲ **A chickadee looks up from its feast of sunflower seeds.**

hand. Stand very, very still and call gently, "Chickadee-dee-dee." It may take a few days of trying before a black-capped friend feels brave enough to visit your hand.

MAKE AN INSECT CAGE

Here's a quick 'n' easy, airy confinement for a captured creature. Observe for a while and then return it to the wild.

YOU NEED

- 2 empty 7½-oz. tuna or cat food cans, tops removed
- A hammer
- A nail
- A felt-tipped marker
- A small piece of scrap wood
- A piece of screen, 7 inches by 12 inches
- String or yarn about 16 inches long
- A large-eyed needle (optional)

TIME OF YEAR

Spring, summer, and fall

Prepare the cans
Take the paper off the cans, make sure there are no sharp edges, and wash thoroughly.

With the marker, put a dot in the center of the inside bottom of each can. Place a can on the piece of scrap wood, and hammer the nail through the bottom, to make a hole. Remove the nail.

Add the screen
Form the screen into a 7-inch-high cylinder which will fit snugly inside the cans (one can on top, one on the bottom). Where the screen overlaps, staple it in three or four places.

Add the string
Tie a knot in one end of the string. Thread it up through the hole in the bottom can (use a large-eyed needle), through the center of the screen cylinder, and up through the hole in the top can. Tie a carrying loop in the top. Make sure there's enough string for an inch or two of play so you can slide up the top can to put in an insect.

Go insect hunting!
Capture a grasshopper, a beetle, or a praying mantis. Add a twig with leaves. Watch for a little while, then let the creature go.

- NOTE: This insect cage is not good for ants or bees. Ants will crawl away through the holes in the screen. Bees may sting you!

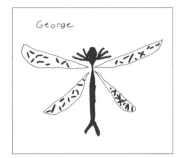
George

◀ **Dragonfly drawing by George Sandquist.**

▼ **Shelley and Michael look at the praying mantis they have captured.**

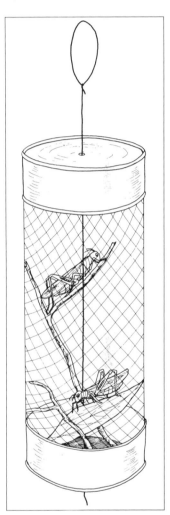

INSECT CAGE

▲ **Two grasshoppers can be observed through the screening.**

CHAPTER 10

LET'S DISCOVER! NATURE'S GARDENS

◀ **A magnifying glass opens up new worlds for Meghann and Karyn.**

▼ **One way to make more dandelions.**

Gardens are all around us.

■ When we walk down a city street, there are gardens of weeds growing between the cracks in the sidewalk, or in vacant lots among rubble.

■ A small patch of woods or an expanse of deep forest is a continually changing garden, with the texture of bark and bud in winter, the small and glorious surprises of wildflowers in spring, the canopy of leaves and understory of ferns in summer, and the harvest of cones, nuts and foliage in autumn.

■ A meadow is a paradise of sun-loving grasses and field flowers, the kind you can pick to use fresh or to dry, without worry of depleting the supply.

■ In a bog, the mat of sphagnum moss supports wild cranberry, cottongrass, delicate pink orchids, and carnivorous plants. Show a child the watery traps in the leaves of pitcher plants, and the red-spiked leaves of sundews that sparkle in summer light before enclosing an insect meal.

■ Walk in an ocean breeze behind sand dunes, savor the blooms of rugosa rose and mallow, and pick beach plums for jam. Beware of poison ivy!

■ Visit a pond and create a tiny plastic-bottomed replica at home, where children can raise frogs and salamanders or make a home for a turtle.

Wherever you walk to enjoy the beauty of nature's gardens, take along your curiosity and a 10x magnifying glass. It opens up new worlds. Tiny flowers or insects that look insignificant can become wondrous when examined up close.

Watch an individual plant or tree grow and change through the seasons. See a milkweed plant push through the ground and produce pink blooms which develop into huge seed pods. Blow the parachuted seeds away when the pods burst in fall. Make friends with a tree. Visit it regularly throughout the year. Discover the plants and animals that live in partnership with it.

Venture out at dawn or dusk to see the world in a different way. Bird song fills the air and frogs croak in full chorus. Wonder about the peepers, the tiny frogs whose night song announces spring, and hear the crickets signal summer's end.

FORAGE FOR WILD FOODS

Forage for wild foods in nature's gardens. Use these as a supplement to the produce of your own garden, or, if you have none, a taste of the incredible flavors of just-picked. This is high adventure to share with a child. Often, the first sighting of a wild food comes by accident, but soon you and the child will learn where to find it.

■ EXERCISE CAUTION. Never let a child pick without checking the identity of a wild food with a knowledgeable adult, and never pick a wild food clean. Leave most of the plants or berries to propagate next year's crop, and for the animals that depend on them for food. Be careful not to trample other plants nearby.

When my children were very young, we often used the reminder "if everybody did . . . ," which came from a humorously illustrated book we had found in the library. If everybody crumpled up just one piece of paper and threw it on the ground, soon the litter would bury us. If everybody picked just a few rare wildflowers, soon there would be none left for others to see. If everybody picked just one small patch of wild leeks clean, there would be none left in no time at all. Think of others who will walk the woods after you and how much they will enjoy what you have seen if you protect it for them.

SPRING— WILD LEEKS

This pungent relative of the cultivated leek smells like a cross between onions and garlic.

Where to find them
Look in rich deciduous woods. Wild leek first pokes up through the ground as a tightly rolled cylinder of leaves. It unfurls to look a little like lily-of-the-valley foliage: two or three smooth, green, pointed ovals, 6 to 9 inches long, attached to an underground bulb. Wild leeks generally grow in large clumps.

What to Do
- DIG, DON'T PULL! Carefully dig out a few bulbs with the trowel. If you try to pull them out, they will break off. Shake off the excess dirt and smell the pungency of the leek. A whole raw leek is too strong for most children, but an adult may enjoy washing off one bulb and eating it right now. (Be prepared for "leek breath" all day!) Pop the rest of the harvest into the plastic bag for the trip home.
- HOW TO SERVE AT HOME. Chop the bulb and the tender part of the green, as you would a scallion, and add to a tossed spring salad. Let children help you use the rest to make Wild Leek and Potato Soup.

YOU NEED
- A plastic bag and twist-tie
- A narrow trowel

TIME OF YEAR
Early spring, when tree leaf buds are just beginning to show green

WILD LEEK
▲ **A wild leek must be dug, not pulled.**

AROMA
◀ **Erin samples the pungent fragrance of this spring vegetable.**

WILD LEEK AND POTATO SOUP

YOU NEED

2   cups wild leeks, washed and thinly sliced (tender green, too)
2   cups potatoes, peeled and thinly sliced or diced
4   cups water (or 2 cups water and 2 cups chicken broth) salt to taste
½   cup milk or cream chopped parsley and chives
■   a potato parer, knife, cutting board, pot, food mill or food processor, and bowl

Simmer together the first four ingredients until the vegetables are tender, about 40 minutes. Puree in a food mill or food processor.

Just before serving, heat again to simmer and add the milk or cream and chopped parsley or chives. Serve, and, as you eat, remember your walk in spring woods!

▲ **The author revels in a walk in the woods in any season.**

SUMMER MYSTERY

In summer, you'll wonder what happened to all the wild leeks you saw in spring. It's a mystery plant! The leaves have disappeared, and the flower stands alone. It's very much like an onion blossom—an umbel of white flowers on a stalk about 12 inches high.

SPRING — FIDDLEHEADS

The tightly curled, emerging fronds of ostrich or cinnamon ferns make a delectable spring vegetable. Did you know that ferns as tall as trees grew when dinosaurs lived on earth?

Where to find them
 ■ OSTRICH FERNS grow in silty flood plains near the banks of rivers and streams. Identify them by last year's dry, fertile frond, which looks like a stiff, brown ostrich feather, standing straight up from the clump.
 ■ CINNAMON FERNS also like wet, soggy places. Their fertile frond appears first in spring, a stiff, thick-stemmed spike, green at first, then cinnamon-colored. The fiddleheads are covered with dense white fuzz that gradually turns brown.

Harvest them
Cut tightly curled fiddleheads at their base when they are less than 6 inches high. Never cut more than one-third of the fiddleheads growing from a clump. *Never cut fiddleheads that have begun to unfurl.* They are no longer edible—in fact, they may be poisonous. Carry your harvest home in the plastic bag.

FIDDLEHEADS

▲ **Cut ostrich fern fiddleheads when they are tightly curled and less than 6 inches high. Harvest only a few from each clump.**

YOU NEED

 ■ A sharp knife
 ■ A plastic bag and twist-tie

TIME OF YEAR

Early spring, when tree leaf buds are just beginning to open

STEAMED FIDDLEHEADS

Steam and serve like asparagus for a taste of spring.

YOU NEED

 ■ Fiddleheads from ostrich or cinnamon ferns
 ■ A basin of water
 ■ A vegetable steamer
 ■ Butter and salt

Wash the fiddleheads thoroughly in the water, removing scales or fuzz. Steam them in a vegetable steamer until tender. Toss with butter, and a tiny sprinkling of salt.

Variation
Cook a few wild leeks with the fiddleheads. Instead of tossing with butter, drizzle with a bit of vinegar, maple syrup, and safflower oil.

SUMMER—
WILD BERRIES

Go berry picking in wild places.

What to look for

■ STRAWBERRIES. Tiny wild strawberries grow in sunny fields and meadows in early summer. Perhaps you'll find some springing up in your own lawn and garden. Pick some to garnish your morning cereal.

■ RASPBERRIES. Brambles invade overgrown fields, spill over roadside ditches, and fill sunny openings in woods. Both black and red raspberries grow wild, maturing in early to midsummer.

■ BLACKBERRIES. Stouter, stiffer canes help you spot these raspberry relatives. Look for them when you pick red raspberries and come back later in summer to harvest when the berries are thoroughly dark.

■ BLUEBERRIES. Find low-growing blueberries among the rocks near mountain tops. Wild highbush varieties often grow in swampy places. Harvesting the big ones always involved wading through muck when I was a child foraging in Long Island woods.

See "Berry Picking for Family Fun," p. 80, for tips on harvesting.

▲ **Greg, Erin, Brian, and Sarah search for tiny wild strawberries in a sunny meadow.**

FALL— WILD GRAPES

Look for wild grapes, which grow abundantly in many places in the U.S. Did you know that the Vikings who first visited our land named it Vinland because of all the wild grapes they found here?

YOU NEED

- Clippers
- A small pail
- A length of rope to go around your waist
- A tall adult to help

TIME OF YEAR

Early fall, before hard frost

Where to find them
Clambering over shrubs and trees in hedgerows, at the edge of woodlands, along streams and riverbanks, in canyon bottoms, or among sand dunes—grapevines grow almost everywhere (except in the northwestern U.S.). The large, roundish, toothed leaves are easy to identify. Don't get grapevines confused with poison ivy, or with Virginia creeper, which has compound leaves.

Harvest them
Tie the pail around your waist with the length of rope, to leave both hands free for tugging at grapevines. Snip off clusters of ripe grapes and drop them into the pail. Some vines may be too high for you to reach. Ask an adult to pull the vine down to you.

SAMPLING

▼ **Ryan samples wild grapes.**

WILD GRAPE JUICE

The secret is never to let the grapes boil. This is a good joint project for children and an adult.

YOU NEED

- A basin of water
- A colander
- A large kettle
- A potato masher
- Water
- A cooking thermometer
- Cheesecloth
- A bowl
- Honey

Wash the grapes thoroughly. Drain them in the colander. Remove grapes from stems and drop into the kettle. Mash with the potato masher to crush the grapes. Add enough water to barely cover them.

Put the thermometer in the grapes. Heat to 160°F and keep at that temperature for 20 minutes. Never let it boil!

Place a double thickness of cheesecloth in the colander and strain the juice through it. Sweeten to taste with honey while still warm.

Refrigerate. Enjoy plain, mixed with seltzer or gingerale, or freeze in ice cube trays, tiny paper cups, or popsicle molds. Insert a popsicle stick before freezing and enjoy a pure wild grape juice popsicle!

- NOTE: If you have made lots of grape juice, a grownup can bottle some to use during the winter. After sweetening, reheat juice to 160°F and pour into hot, sterilized jars. Process in a boiling water bath for 5 minutes.

GO FOR A WALK IN THE WOODS

Take a walk in the woods with a child. Share its wonder together. Play a game to increase awareness. "So many people look but never see," says a friend of mine. Discover what is all around you.

LOOK!

▲ **"Over here, Trevor! We see a frog."** Use a net to scoop up pond life for a quick examination.

With a very young child, look for colors or shapes or textures. How many shades of green can you find? How many white things, red things, blue things? How many round things, square things, triangular things? Find something that is hard, soft, pointy, or slimy.

Help an older child to identify some common wildflowers (see p. 157). Teach children to look but never pick. Many wildflowers are endangered species, and are protected by law. Help to ensure their presence for future generations of children.

Collect tree leaves in summer or fall. Press them. Younger children can match similar shapes, or classify leaves according to shape, size, or vein structure. Older children can use a simple field guide to find out names of trees, identified by leaves, bark, general shape, and bud arrangement. All children enjoy art projects with leaves. Place them between sheets of waxed paper and iron, make leaf books, leaf prints, leaf skeletons, or leaf people.

Animals of the forest are of great interest to children, but they're seldom visible

when chattery youngsters walk in the woods. Look for signs of life, and conduct a friendly contest to become aware of the teeming life that is a part of a forest ecosystem. (On a spring field trip, my first graders found sixty DIFFERENT signs of life!)

Discover holes—holes in leaves, holes in bark, holes in tree trunks, holes in the ground. Try to figure out who made the holes and why. Cone scales and cone cores deposited on the ground tell a red squirrel's been busy feasting on its seeds. Look for signs of

▼ **A red eft is the "teenage" stage of the spotted salamander. Chris found this one under some leaves.**

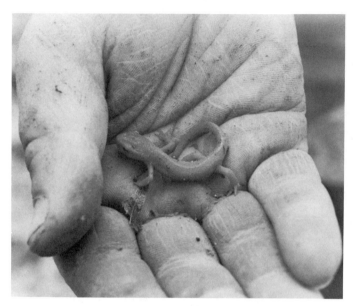

Only look at what is to be seen, and you will have garden enough, without deepening the soil in your yard. We have only to elevate our view a little, to see the whole forest as a garden.

HENRY DAVID THOREAU

Henry David Thoreau, "Autumnal Tints," The Natural History Essays *(Salt Lake City: Gibbs M. Smith, Inc., Peregrine Smith Books, 1984), p. 172.*

beaver—dams, lodges, and gnawed trees with the signatures of their teeth. Discover where porcupines have nibbled the bark of trees. Find ant hills, insect galls, and bird feathers. Turn over a rotting log, and see who lives underneath. Listen for sounds—the chirp of a chipmunk, the chatter of chickadee, the call of crow or raven. In winter, follow the patterns of tracks in snow, and see where they lead you.

Forays into woods can be satisfying in themselves. Sometimes they may inspire gardening projects at home.

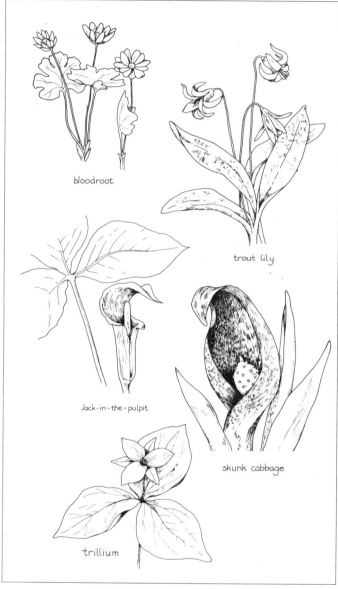

bloodroot

trout lily

Jack-in-the-pulpit

skunk cabbage

trillium

TRILLIUM
▼ Celisa looks closely at a white trillium.

MAKE FIVE WILDFLOWER FRIENDS

A walk in early spring woods is like a walk in a garden. Under the light shade of deciduous trees just beginning to leaf, wildflowers bloom in the coolness of early spring sunshine. Children and adults can enjoy them without knowing their names, but it is like visiting friends when you learn the names of a few easily identified flowers.

WARNING! Look, but do not pick. Many wildflowers are endangered and pro-

YOU NEED

- Curiosity
- A magnifying glass, preferably 10x
- A wildflower guide (optional)

TIME OF YEAR

Early spring

tected by law, and many will die immediately once they are picked. Explain this to children BEFORE you go to the woods.

Look for two early bloomers
- SKUNK CABBAGE. Look in a swampy place for the flower of skunk cabbage, which pushes up from winter sleep even before the leaves emerge. It looks like a purple hood surrounding a green, pineapple-like inner cylinder. Later, the 2-foot-high green leaves fill damp lowlands in the forest. Crush part of a leaf and learn why it's called skunk cabbage!

- BLOODROOT. Look for white, star-like, many-petalled flowers about an inch across in open deciduous woods in very early spring. They are elusive, unfolding only in sunshine and closing up whenever it fades. Soon the leaves that are furled around the flower stems will open and grow large, and that's when you really know you've found bloodroot. The leaves are wonderful, full of indentations that look a bit like the fiords of Norway. Bloodroot lives up to its name. The juice from its roots and stems runs red. Indians used it for dye.

SKUNK CABBAGE

▲ "Phew! Now I know why this is named skunk cabbage," says Greg. (Skunk cabbage is abundant, but most other wildflowers should NOT be picked!)

Learn two T's

■ TROUT LILY (also called Adder's Tongue, Dog-Tooth Violet, or Fawn Lily). The leaves of trout lily are mottled with purple, and look very much like the side of a fish. From the center of a pair of leaves rises a stalk with a nodding, bell-shaped yellow bloom. Trout lily carpets whole areas of early spring woods. As the leaves mature, they lose their purple mottling, and disappear completely by early summer.

■ TRILLIUM. A tricycle has three wheels, a triangle has three sides, triplets are three children born to the same mother at the same time, a trio consists of three musicians, and trillium has three leaves, three sepals, and three petals.

There are several varieties of trillium. Most spectacular are the large drifts of white trillium that carpet deciduous woods.

The blossoms turn pink as the flowers age.

A bit harder to spot are the nodding maroon blooms of red trillium, or wake-robin. When you get close, you'll find out the flower emits an unpleasant odor, as of meat gone bad. In fact, some people call it Stinking Willie. This attracts the big green fleshfly, red trillium's main pollinator.

Painted trillium is rarer. It grows in the soil of acid woods. The small white bloom has red blazes at the base of each petal, as though someone touched it with a paintbrush.

Find the little man of the forest

■ JACK-IN-THE-PULPIT. Find this a bit later in spring than its cousin, the skunk cabbage. Children should be able to see the family resemblance in the flower—a striped, sheath-like hood, or

"pulpit," with Jack inside preaching. Spot a Jack-in-the pulpit by the one or two sets of large leaves, each divided into three leaflets, which tower above the flower. The plant grows 2 to 3 feet tall in moist woods. After the leaves have withered in summer, if you're alert, you may see the flower stalk, topped with a brilliant cluster of red berries. That's what's left of Jack.

This is just a sampling of spring wildflowers in deciduous woods, all fairly common, and distinct in name and shape. After you master these, add to your list. Look for marsh marigold, Dutchman's breeches and squirrel corn, spring beauty, wild ginger, toothwort, foamflower, Solomon's seal, and lady's-slipper (a wild orchid). Once you're hooked, you'll always be trying to learn one more!

▼ Planting plan, Woodland Wildflower Garden

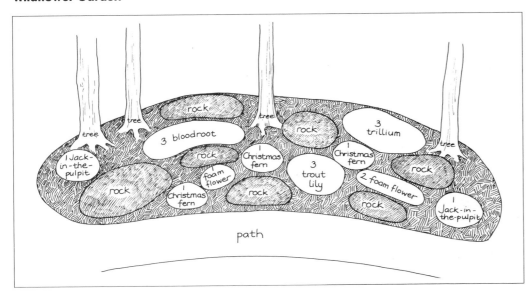

Labels within image: tree, tree, tree, tree, rock, 3 bloodroot, 1 Jack-in-the-pulpit, rock, rock, 1 foam flower, 1 Christmas fern, 1 Christmas fern, rock, 3 trout lily, rock, rock, 3 trillium, 1 Christmas fern, 2 foam flower, rock, rock, 1 Jack-in-the-pulpit, path

START A WOODLAND WILDFLOWER GARDEN

A child who has enjoyed the flowers of spring woods can grow a few easy-to-raise favorites at home, along with evergreen Christmas fern. (Some of these plants may not bloom for a season or more after planting.)

CAUTION! This project can be successful only if you have a habitat similar to that in which these flowers grow in the wild. Note what trees and shrubs grow with them in the woods. You need a patch of deciduous woods with soil rich in leaf mold, or a shady spot under small trees and a willingness to prepare the soil to meet plant needs.

Never dig plants from the wild. Buy them from a reputable wildflower nursery.

Make woods soil
Spread a layer several inches thick of leaf mold, peat moss, and compost on the planting area. Dig it into the soil. Use enough so the earth feels as spongy as forest soil. Dig some sand into the places reserved for trillium.

Add rocks and a path
Roll some rocks into place, according to the garden plan. They'll give structure to the garden and serve as stepping stones, so you won't walk on the soil and compact it. This is definitely a job to do with a grownup!

Put a thick layer of shredded bark or pine needles on the path. If you lay plastic on the ground first, you'll have less trouble with weeds.

Plant the ferns and wildflowers
Dig planting holes, set the wildflowers and ferns in the ground at the same level they grew in the nursery, and firm the soil around them. Trout lily are the hardest of this group to transplant. Make sure there's really deep leaf mold for them.

Water
Remember, these plants like cool, damp, and shady woods. Water well after planting and keep them moist until they are well established.

Add a forest carpet
Add a layer of mulch— chopped leaves, pine needles, or shredded bark. Before winter, add an extra inch or two of leaves or pine needles as winter cover. If your plants like their new home, they should multiply and thrive, as long as you give them moisture, and add another layer of "forest litter" for protection and nourishment each spring and fall.

▼ **Woods soil, gravel, charcoal, mosses, ferns, and an evergreen seedling are the ingredients for a woodland terrarium.**

TERRARIUM CONTAINERS

A woodland terrarium

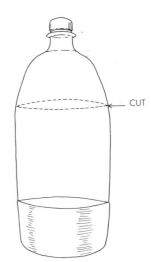

A jungle terrarium

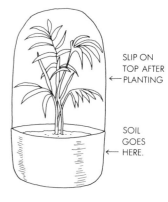

← CUT

SLIP ON
TOP AFTER
← PLANTING

SOIL
GOES
← HERE.

Any clear glass container can become a home for one plant or many:
A fishbowl
A brandy snifter
An aquarium (add a pane of glass for a cover)
A candy glass or cookie jar

An apothecary jar
An old mason jar with glass cover
A plastic soda bottle (Separate base. Cut clear top where it begins to curve. Turn upside-down and fit into base.)

MAKE A WOODLAND TERRARIUM

Recreate a tiny forest habitat inside a jar, to remind you of autumn woods all winter. This is a place for the fairies to dance!

Create the foundation
Turn the jar on its side. Put a small wedge of wood or a piece of plasticene clay on either side to keep it from rolling. The foundation should fill the bottom quarter of the jar, and there should be half as much drainage material as soil. In the bottom of the jar, put 3 parts gravel or small pebbles and 1 part crushed charcoal.

Cut the nylon stocking to fit the jar, and place it on top of the drainage layer. It will act as a soil separator, to keep soil from washing down into the drainage layer.

Add potting soil or woods soil on top of the stocking, to fill the bottom quarter of the jar. Use a stick or long-handled spoon to create a landscape of hills and valleys with the soil.

Make a fairy garden
Start at the base of the jar and work toward the mouth. Plant the tallest plants first, then low ones, and finally the mosses and lichens. Pixie cup seems especially suited for a fairy garden! Add rocks or moss-covered twigs for fairy seats.

Water sparingly
Drizzle a bit of water near each plant with a medicine dropper, a long-handled spoon, or a long-spouted watering can. If water or soil spatters on the glass, swab it with a tissue.

ROUND AND ROUND

A terrarium creates a miniature water cycle. Water is taken up by plants from the soil, lost through their leaves (that's called transpiration), condenses on the sides of the terrarium, and runs down to water the soil again, similar to the water cycle in the larger world.

Charitable Trusts Can Make Capital Gains Taxes Optional

by Mike Winter

Are you thinking of selling a home, vacation home, raw land, stocks, or other appreciated property? Whether real estate or securities, if you've owned the asset for more than one year and the value has increased significantly over what you paid, you will be paying capital gains taxes.

If you are thinking of selling, you may want to consider placing the property in a charitable remainder trust (CRT). Here's why. Once the property is placed in the CRT, it can be sold without incurring income tax on the capital gains. The entire proceeds, less selling costs, can then be invested to provide a stream of income to you as the lifetime income beneficiary of the trust.

What is a CRT? A CRT is an agreement in which a donor transfers assets to a trustee who invests the assets in a separate fund. The beneficiary of the trust receives income each year equal to a percentage of the fair market value of the trust assets. At the end of the trust period, usually at the death of the income recipients, whatever remains in the trust is distributed to charity.

Since the CRT is an irrevocable (nonreversible) transfer of property and the remainder eventually goes to charity, there is also an immediate income tax deduction. If the deduction can't be used up in the first year, the IRS allows five additional years.

Here's an example of a situation in which a CRT might be considered. A couple, Mr. and Mrs. Blessed, ages 68 and 67, are considering selling appreciated stocks. They paid $30,000 for the stock many years ago. It will sell for approximately $150,000 today. The difference between the cost of the stock and the net selling price (after selling costs) is $120,000. If the Blesseds are in the 28 percent tax bracket, they will pay $33,600 in capital gains taxes. Thus the net amount remaining for investment is $86,400. Investing conservatively with a 6 percent return, the Blesseds will receive $5,184 in annual income.

If the Blesseds desire to remember charity with a part of their estate anyway, they might consider a CRT. They create a trust, give their stock to the trust, and the trust sells it. Here are the results: an immediate income tax deduction of $51,672, capital gains taxes of $33,600 are avoided, lifetime

Over the next 22 years (the Blesseds' government-expected life span), total income to the Blesseds will total more than $245,000. Finally, at the death of the survivor of Mr. or Mrs. Blessed, the amount remaining will go to charity. Since the charity is tax exempt, in most cases, the capital gains taxes are never paid.

To learn more about the CRT, please call me, Mike Winter, at 708/260-4900 or 1-800-979-2828, or return the coupon and we will provide you with additional information.

Yes, I'm interested in learning more about how to make capital gains taxes optional.

❏ Please send me more information about Charitable Remainder Trusts.

Name(s) _____

Address _____

City _____ State _____ ZIP _____

Telephone _____

❏ Please send me a detailed illustration of a CRT.

Birth date _____ Spouse's birth date _____

Property description _____

Be Part of the Solution

Today's technology brings us instant news from around the world. Minutes after a crisis tears through a country, we know about the tragedy.

And just as quickly as we hear about a tragedy, CBInternational is prepared to respond through our Good Samaritan Program. Wherever a crisis occurs, from Dakar to Donetsk, your gifts enable us to speed compassion and comfort to your neighbors all around the world. Through Good Samaritan funds, we can powerfully demonstrate Christ's love in a practical way.

Good Samaritan funds helped us team with World Relief to provide blankets and bowls, rice and beans to Rwandans crowded into refugee camps.

As homeless victims of the Kobe quake in Japan trembled in the streets, Good Samaritan funds brought them food and shelter.

And recently, your gifts to the Good Samaritan Fund helped save young lives in Donetsk, Ukraine, by providing an incubator for a severely under-equipped hospital that serves millions.

"If the parents could thank you, they would write it in tears," said Dr. Valentina Podolyaka, director of the hospital.

Right now, CBI is focusing on other Good Samaritan Fund needs in the Ukraine. We are praying for $25,000 to help us provide 10 wheelchairs, four incubators, and a container of basic medical supplies.

Won't you please pray about how the Lord might use you in touching the lives of your neighbors in Ukraine and all around the world?

To give, make checks payable to CBInternational or CBI, mark them for the Good Samaritan Fund, and mail to: CBInternational, P.O. Box 5, Wheaton, IL 60189-0005.

Thank you so much for helping us show Christ's compassionate love in a practical way.

Be a Good Samaritan… Help Heal the World.

▼ **Brooks gazes at his newly planted terrarium.**

YOU NEED

- A clean, wide-mouth gallon jar (you should be able to get your hands inside)
- Gravel or small pebbles
- Crushed charcoal
- An old nylon stocking
- Humusy potting soil or woods soil
- A small rock or stone, and/or moss-covered twigs
- Tiny woodland plants, such as:
  - an evergreen seedling
  - a fern or small plants
  - mosses and lichens (pixie cup if you can find it)
- A medicine dropper or long-handled spoon or a watering can with long spout
- Plastic wrap

CAUTION: Do not dig up any plants that are on your state conservation list.

TIME OF YEAR

Autumn

A mini-greenhouse

Cover the open end of the jar with a piece of plastic wrap, held in place with a rubber band. Punch a few holes in it. Set the terrarium in shade for a day while the plants adjust. If the inside fogs up, open the plastic wrap for a few hours. If the mosses seem dry, drizzle a bit of water over them. Once you have the right amount of moisture, the terrarium should take care of itself and you shouldn't need to water it. Put it in an east or north window, where it will get light but no direct sun.

VARIATION

Use tiny jungle plants (sold as houseplants) instead of woodland plants. They, too, thrive in an environment with high humidity.

Try any of these: calathea, Chinese evergreen, cryptanthus, dwarf dracaena, dwarf palm, ferns, fittonia, maranta, pepperomia, pileas (artillery plant, creeping Charlie, watermelon pilea), or small-leaved philodendron.

FROM FOREST TO DESERT— MAKE A DESERT DISH GARDEN

Woodland plants thrive in shady, damp places. Show how different an ecosystem can be by creating a desert habitat for plants that grow in hot, sunny places with little rainfall.

YOU NEED

- A container: use a wide clay bulb pot, or raid the kitchen for:
    - A shallow casserole
    - A soup bowl
    - A ceramic tumbler
    - A divided canape dish
- Stones or crockery
- Gravel
- Crushed charcoal
- Potting mix: buy a commercial cactus mix, or make your own from:
    - 1 part commercial potting soil
    - 1 part sharp sand (aquarium sand or builders sand)
    - ½ part crushed charcoal
    - 1 tablespoon ground limestone
    - 1 tablespoon bone meal for each gallon of mix
- Assorted cacti
- A rock or small piece of driftwood (optional)
- Extra sand or pebbles (optional)
- A blunt stick
- A small trowel or a spoon
- A watering can

TIME OF YEAR

Any time

Cacti are specially fitted to survive in a desert. Their stems store water to carry them through long periods when there is no rainfall. They have weapons—prickly spines—to keep away animals that might feast on their juicy flesh. The cacti need all that stored water for themselves!

Cacti are easy to grow, which makes them perfect for a child's project. They thrive on dry air and neglect—infrequent watering, yearly feeding, and, because they grow slowly, little repotting. They have few insect enemies. They DO need lots of light and a porous soil.

Build a drainage system
In the bottom of the container, put a layer of stones or crockery. Next, add a layer of coarse gravel and a shallow layer of crushed charcoal. Add some potting mix.

Landscape the garden
Place the cactus plants in the dish garden in a pleasing arrangement. They'll look best if you leave plenty of space between groupings. Don't crowd the container.

Watch out for those spines! Wear gloves to protect tender fingers, and use a folded sling of newspaper or cloth to help you hold on to each cactus without being pricked.

Fill in around the cacti with potting mix, tamping firmly with a blunt stick. For a neat, deserty look, cover

NEAT NAMES

Here's a sampler of cacti names:

pin cushion	Bishop's cap
rat tail	barrel
thimble	strawberry
rabbit ear	pink pearl
fish hook	Old Man of the Andes
organ pipe	fire crown
hedgehog	owl's eyes
popcorn	lobster claw
boxing glove	rattlesnake
prickly pear	peanut
rambling ranchero	chalk candle

the top of the potting mix with extra gravel or pebbles. Add a pretty stone or a small piece of driftwood for an accent.

What about water?
Do not water at all for three or four days. This helps the roots to heal. Then water thoroughly.

After that, water only when the soil is COMPLETELY dry. In winter, cacti rest. They need water even

DESERT DISH GARDEN

▲ **Karyn's desert dish garden contains an assortment of cacti and succulents.**

less often—once every two or three weeks.

Never water when it is raining, but instead only on dry days, preferably in the morning. Use warm water. Cold water shocks this desert plant!

A place to grow
Put your dish garden where it will get plenty of light—in a south window, or under artificial light.

The desert in spring is a fantastic garden, with the blooms of cacti ablaze like a flamboyant celebration before summer heat arrives.

If you want to encourage your dish-garden cacti to bloom in spring, hold back water in winter, and make sure they have cool temperatures at that time—40 to 45°F at night and no more than 65°F during the day. If the cacti are under artificial light, try to have the number of light hours match the lengthening days of spring.

ROMP IN A MEADOW

Romp with a child in the high grass of a meadow. Discover the plants and animals that live in this sunny, open place.

In June, look for spittle bugs under the foam children call "snake spit." Find woodchuck holes and count the entrances and exits. (My first graders found a woodchuck apartment complex with more than ten ins and outs!) Blow away the parachuted seeds of dandelions and make a wish. Look at hawks soaring overhead. Turn over a rock and see who lives underneath. Count the different kinds of grasses you can see.

In late summer, listen to the buzz-hum of insects. Watch grasshoppers explode from the grass as you walk through it. Find garden spiders waiting for dinner. Look in a milkweed patch for yellow, black, and white-striped caterpillars. Give one a home in an airy cage (see p. 146), with milkweed leaves to eat. Watch the miracle of its transformation into a pale green chrysalis dotted with gold, which in a couple of weeks will become black, then transparent, as a monarch butterfly emerges. Let its wings dry, and release it to feed on flower nectar and prepare for a long migration southward to Central America.

On a dry day in late fall, let children pull long wool socks over their shoes, and run through a field. See what sticks to the socks—an assortment of seeds for another year's growth, designed to travel on the coats of animals and people to new locations.

▲ Celisa's leg disappears into a woodchuck hole.

▲ A romp in a meadow is a joyous thing! (l. to r.: Nicole, Greg, Chris, Celisa, Brian, and Erin)

MEADOW DESIGNS

Collect and press leaves, grasses, and delicate meadow flowers. Us them to make a sunprint, stationery, or a bookmark.

YOU NEED

- Leaves, flowers, and/or grasses
- Newsprint or newspapers
- Heavy books

TIME OF YEAR

Spring and summer

PRESSING

▲ **To press leaves and flowers, place them carefully between several sheets of newsprint, weigh down with books, and leave for a week or two.**

HOW TO PRESS LEAVES AND FLOWERS

Collect small, thin flowers, leaves, and grasses for best results. A violet, for instance, presses more satisfactorily than a dandelion does. Ferns sometimes grow in a hedgerow at the edge of a meadow, and they press well, too.

Spread out the collected materials on thick pads of newsprint. Make sure there are no curled edges on leaves or flowers.

Stack the newsprint pads and weigh down with a pile of heavy books. Leave for about two weeks. When the materials are thoroughly dry, you are ready for some fun.

MAKE A SUNPRINT

The sun works magic for you. All you need to provide is some special photographic paper and fixer.

Mix the fixer
Mix the fixer according to manufacturer's directions. Do this several hours before you plan to make the sunprints, so it will have time to cool to room temperature.

Make a holder
Tape the glass to the cardboard along one edge to make a "book." This will hold the special paper and the meadow plants while the

sun does its work. Clean the glass thoroughly.

Pull the shades and begin
Sunprint paper must be kept out of bright light. Pull the shades and turn off the lights.

Make your design
Open the glass book and place the sunprint paper, glossy side up, on the cardboard. Arrange pressed grasses, leaves, and flowers on the paper to make a pleasing design. Don't be in a hurry! Try a few arrangements and decide what looks best. Close the glass to hold everything in place.

Magic time!
Hold the glass book tightly on the corners opposite the taped edge. Make sure your thumbs do not cover the paper.

Go outside and let the sun shine directly on the book. Watch what happens! The sunprint paper turns purple, then dark brown. When it looks almost black (after 3 or 4 minutes), go back inside.

Voila!
Keep the windowshades down and the lights turned off. Open the glass and remove the plants. Wow! Isn't that beautiful! (If you want to make more sunprints, put this one between the pages of a book or in a black plastic bag until you're done exposing the rest to sunlight.)

Fix the sunprints
What would happen if you

YOU NEED

- A sunny day (THIS WILL NOT WORK ON AN OVERCAST DAY!)
- Kodak Professional Studio Proof Paper (called P.O.P. or printing-out-paper) single weight, white, smooth, glossy (It comes 8 inches by 10 inches. You may want to cut it into 4 pieces.)
- A pane of glass an inch or two larger than the paper (Make sure sharp edges have been ground smooth.)
- A piece of heavy cardboard the same size as the glass
- A piece of cloth tape
- Pressed and dried leaves, flowers, and grasses
- Photographic fixer for black-and-white prints, in solution
- A plastic or stainless-steel tray larger than the sunprint paper
- Tongs
- Water and a sink
- A new sponge

TIME OF YEAR

Spring and summer

SUNPRINTS

▲ **Nicole carefully arranges dried leaves and grasses on the photographic paper before closing the glass book to hold the materials in place.**

◀ **Sunlight makes magical changes! See how the paper has darkened in just three minutes.**

took your beautiful sunprint outdoors? The paper would turn completely dark. In order to preserve the design, you must "fix" the print.

Pour prepared fixer solution into the tray. Slide in your sunprint(s). With the tongs, agitate the solution gently. Make sure the sunprint paper is completely under the fixer.

If you've used powdered fixer, keep the sunprints in the solution for 10 minutes. With liquid mix, 3 or 4 minutes is long enough.

Wash the sunprints
Fill a sink or large dishpan with water at a temperature of 65° to 75°F. Add the sunprint(s). Keep the faucet running slowly into the basin and let the prints wash for 30 minutes.

Dry the sunprints
Lay the sunprints face up on a blotter of paper towels. With a thoroughly rinsed new sponge, gently blot the excess water from the prints.

Flatten the sunprints
Let the prints air dry. They will curl slightly. To flatten them, place between sheets of white paper and iron face down.

How to use them
Mat and hang on the wall. Glue or dry-mount prints to greeting cards. Send special greetings to your favorite friends and relatives.

EXPOSING

▲ **First graders expose their sunprints. They press the glass tightly against the cardboard backing to keep their designs from shifting.**

◀ **Nicole's finished sunprint.**

▼ **Lindsay cuts the contact paper up to the corner of the note paper so it can be folded under.**

MAKE PRESSED FLOWER NOTE PAPER

Pressed and dried meadow plants themselves make lovely greeting cards.

Make the design
Arrange the pressed plant materials into a pleasing design on the greeting card. You can even recreate a meadow scene!

Add contact paper
Peel the backing from the contact paper. Position it over the design so that the edges of the contact paper extend ½ inch beyond the edges of the folded card. Press the contact against the note card to hold the pressed plants in place. Rub with your hand from the center to the edges to make it adhere, pressing out air bubbles.

With a scissors, cut the bottom two corners of the contact paper at a 45° angle, into the card. Cut the top edge in line with the fold.

Fold over the edges of the contact paper, smooth it with your fingers, and cut off any protruding corners. Done!

YOU NEED

- Pressed and dried flowers, leaves, and/or grasses
- Clear contact paper, cut into 6-inch by 7-inch pieces
- 6-inch by 10-inch heavyweight paper for greeting cards, folded in half
- Scissors

TIME OF YEAR

Spring and summer

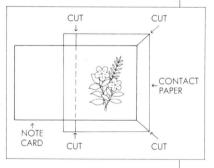

VARIATIONS

Change the size of the note paper. Just cut the clear contact paper so there is a ½-inch overlap on each edge.

Use the same process to make bookmarks, place cards, or placemats.

▶ **Pressed flower note paper is a lovely remembrance of a romp in a meadow.**

CHAPTER 11

LET'S DISCOVER! PLANT EXPERIMENTS

For those who wonder how and why seeds sprout, how to grow a garden without seeds, and how liquids travel in plants.

WHY DO PLANTS NEED SUN?

Plants use the energy from sunlight to manufacture their food.

SEED MIRACLES

Cover a seed with earth. Wait and wonder. What's happening in the darkness underground?

Here are ways to give a child a peek at the mystery and wonder of seed miracles—of the tiny embryo imbedded in the seed package, of its bursting out of that package as germination begins.

WHAT'S IN A SEED?

Make a square of dry beans
Arrange the seeds on the paper in three rows of three to make a square, each seed touching its neighbors. Trace around the outside of the beans. Label the square "dry beans."

Soak the beans
Put the bean seeds in the glass of water and let them soak overnight. Arrange the soaked seeds on the paper in the same way you laid them out dry. Trace around them. Label the square "wet beans." Which takes up more space, dry beans or soaked beans? Why?

Open a bean
Very carefully, peel off the bean's seed coat—its skin—and separate the two halves of the seed. These are called cotyledons. They feed the plant until it can make food for itself. Look for the tiny plant, curled up and ready to grow, at the top of one cotyledon. The magnifying glass will help you find miniature leaves, stem, and a root. This is the embryo. Make a drawing to help you

Photo by Linda Tilgner

remember what you have discovered.

Plant some beans
Plant a few beans in soil, or in a seed viewer. Watch the stem emerge as a loop and unbend to carry the cotyledons right up out of

the soil, and see the leaves unfold from it! If you keep your lima bean plant in a warm and sunny place, water it, and feed it, it will make more lima bean seeds to plant next year. Leave the pods on the plant until they are dry.

WHAT'S INSIDE?

▲ **Trevor peels the seed coat from a lima bean that has been soaked in water overnight.**

▼ **Karyn admires the plant she grew from a lima bean seed.**

▼ **A seed pod develops from a flower on this lima bean plant.**

AFTER SOAKING BEANS:

JARED: "Of course they got bigger. I knew. They soak the water up so the little seed can pop out."

DAVID: "I'm going to test them in the old place (the space the dry beans filled). I could only fit two rows of three in the old space."

YOU NEED

- 9 lima bean seeds
- A glass of water
- Pencil and paper
- A magnifying glass

TIME OF YEAR

Any time

TIME NEEDED

Overnight

WHY DO PLANTS AND PEOPLE GROW?

Plants and people are made of cells. When cells divide and multiply, plants and people grow. Their growth is "programmed," in much the same way as a computer is programmed, by genes passed on to them by their parents. Plants and people need food as fuel for growth, and because they live, someday they will die.

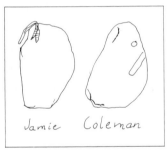

▲ **Lima bean drawn by Jamie Coleman**

SEED EXPLOSIONS

Watch the underground explosions that occur after you plant radish seeds or tiny seeds of lettuce or cress. Find out about root hairs!

Plant the seeds
Fold a tissue so it fits into the bottom of the petri dish or jar lid. Sprinkle about ten seeds on top of the tissue. Spray the seeds and tissue with water until the tissue is thoroughly moist. Cover the petri dish, or set the plastic tumbler upside-down over the jar lid.

Keep watch
Look at the seeds a few times each day. By the next day, the seed coats should begin to crack. After that, the roots will begin to push out. Did all the seeds sprout?
　　Watch for the big explosion of root hairs. Each root will look like a ball of fuzz for a few hours. What do root hairs do? They absorb nutrients and water from the soil. The root hairs will seem to disappear as the stem and leaves emerge. Actually, new ones keep forming on the growing tip of the root.

What next?
Keep spraying the tissue to keep it moist. Watch the roots grow right into it. Your plants will be strong enough to push the cover off the petri dish as they grow! Move half the seedlings to soil and see how they fare compared to the ones left in the petri dish. Can you figure out why?

Photo by Linda Tilgner

YOU NEED

- Tiny seeds (Radishes are most spectacular, but lettuce or garden cress will also give a show.)
- Facial tissues
- A petri dish with cover or a jar lid and a plastic tumbler
- Water
- A spray-misting bottle

TIME OF YEAR

Any time

TIME NEEDED

A few days

SPROUTS

▲ **Paddy inspects cress seeds sprouting in a petri dish. "The root hairs grew right into the tissue! They must be super strong,"** he says.

SPRAYING

▼ **Brian sprays the lettuce he transplanted from the petri dish.**

AFTER ONE DAY

"Yesterday our seeds were all black. Today they're white and brown."

"They look like little vines, like a big huge shield, like tubes ticking out of the root, like needles."

RAPID GROWER

◄ **Within a few days, radish roots have grown fast. You may even see tiny root hairs.**

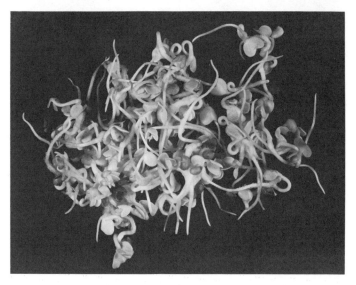

▼ **No matter how they're planted, the roots end up going down. These corn seeds have just been planted in the seed viewer.**

YOU NEED

- A tall glass or jar with straight sides, at least 4 inches tall
- Construction paper or blotting paper, in a dark color, to fit around the inside of the glass
- Paper towels
- 4 or 5 large seeds
- Construction paper to make a collar
- Water

TIME OF YEAR

Any time

TIME NEEDED

About two weeks

MAKE A SEED VIEWER

Watch the germination of large seeds, such as corn, beans, pumpkin, and peas.

Make the viewer
Line the inside of the glass with construction paper or blotting paper. Crumple up some paper towels, one at a time, and fill the glass inside the construction paper with them. Trim the top edge of the construction paper so it is even with the top of the glass.

Plant the seeds
Carefully slip each seed between the glass and construction paper until it is an inch to an inch and a half below the top edge of the glass. Slowly pour water into the center of the paper towels until the construction or blotting paper is completely wet.

Darkness, please!
Make a collar for your viewer so that the seeds will be in the dark. Use construction paper an inch taller than the glass and long enough to form a cylinder that will slip loosely over it. First write your name, the type of seed, and the date of planting on the paper, then staple it into a cylinder.

Watch the miracle
Set the seed viewer on a sunny windowsill and slip on the collar. Lift the collar at the same time each day to see what is happening. Add

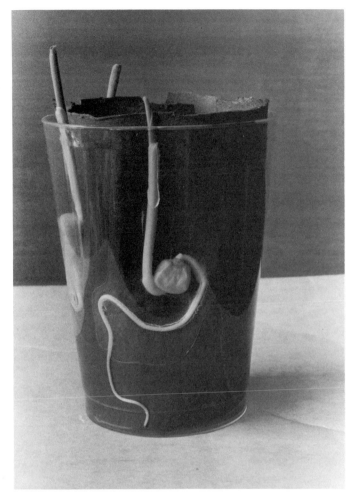

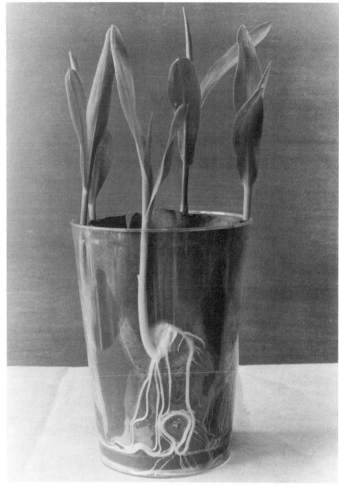

AFTER FOUR DAYS

◀ **CHRIS: "We have root hairs! They're fuzzy."**

JARED: "I discovered something interesting. If you just put them in dirt, you couldn't see this: When the root hairs grow, the stem begins to grow."

AFTER NINE DAYS

▲ **KARYN: "Look! Look! The stem went past the top of the glass!"**

water as needed to keep paper towels moist. You will see the seed swell as it soaks up water, watch the seed coat crack and the root emerge and grow. Next out comes the stem, and finally, the leaves. When you plant a seed in soil, all these wonders occur below the ground, shrouded in mystery. Isn't it exciting to watch?

What next?
After leaves have formed, transplant half of the seedlings to a 4-inch (or larger) pot and fill with potting soil or planting mix. Water well and set in a sunny spot. Continue to keep the paper towels in the seed viewer wet. What happens to the seedlings in each environment after one week? After two weeks?

AFTER TWELVE DAYS

▲ **ERIN: "The root's getting so long it doesn't have enough room. It goes all around the bottom. The glass is blocking it in."**

KARYN: "My roots are all tangled up."

MAKE A GROWTH GRAPH

How fast does a seed grow? Chart the growth of the stems from the seeds in your seed viewer.

Measure

When the stem first emerges from the seed in the seed viewer, hold a piece of paper tape against the outside of the glass so that the bottom of the tape is lined up with the bottom of the stem. Ask a friend to make a pencil mark even with the top of the stem. Cut the paper tape on the mark and label it with the date. Measure the same plant at the same time each day for a week or more.

Assemble

Each day, glue or paste your measured strip on a piece of construction paper. Make sure the bottom edges of all the strips are even. Predict how much longer the next day's strip will be. Think of a good title for your graph. If you like, use a ruler to measure the height of each strip.

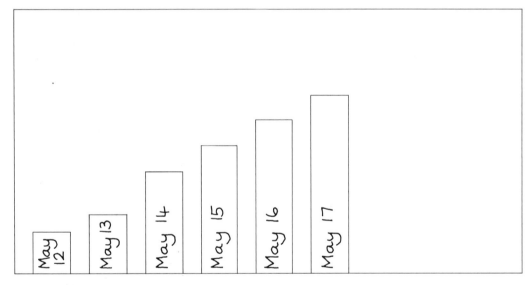

GROWTH GRAPH

▲ **This growth graph shows the development of a corn seedling in a seed viewer.**

▶ **Lindsay cuts a paper strip to match the height of her corn plant.**

VEGGIE PROPAGATION: PLANTS FROM PARTS

You don't need a seed in order to grow a plant. Here's how to use part of an old plant to grow a new one. Call this garbage gardening!

MAKE A CARROT OR BEET-TOP DISH GARDEN

YOU NEED

- A few beets and/or carrots
- A knife and cutting board
- A shallow dish
- Sand or small pebbles
- Water

TIME OF YEAR

Any time

TIME NEEDED

Two to three weeks

Cut
Cut off the top of each beet and carrot with about 1 inch of vegetable. (Eat the rest for supper.)

Plant
Fill the shallow dish with sand or small pebbles. Stick the cut carrot and beet tops into the sand or pebbles. Add water so that the cut surfaces are covered and the crowns are above water.

Watch
Put the dish in a place with good light but no direct sun. Make sure there is always enough water in the dish to cover the bottoms of the veggies. In about a week, new leaves should start to sprout from the veggie tops. You've just made a great centerpiece for the kitchen table! It should last for three or four weeks.

BEET TOPS

▲ **Beet tops sprout in a dish garden.**

GROW A PINEAPPLE PLANT

A pineapple plant is a BROMELIAD. It is related to the air plants that attach themselves to the bark of jungle trees (see p. 198). You need patience for this project.

Cut
Cut off the top of a pineapple with about an inch of fruit attached. Let it air dry for a day or two.

Plant
Put some crockery in the bottom of the flower pot and partially fill it with moistened planting mix mixed with sand and a handful of coffee grounds. Set the pineapple top in place and cover the fruit with soil, so that only the crown of leaves shows above the soil. Firm the soil, and water well.

Be patient
Set the pot in a sunny, warm spot. Keep the soil moist but not sodden. When you water, pour the liquid right into the crown of the plant. Bromeliads take in water and food through their leaves. It may take a couple of months before the pineapple shows any signs of growth. Cheer when you see new green leaves emerging from the center of the crown.

What next?
Keep watering when soil seems dry. Spray half-strength liquid fertilizer into the leaf whorl weekly.

Would you like to persuade the pineapple plant to flower and fruit? Put a few pieces of cut apple in the flower pot. Slip the potted plant into a plastic bag and secure it with a twist tie. Leave for four or five days. The apple gives off ethylene gas. If you are lucky, it might induce the plant to bloom. Watch the flower develop into a tiny pineapple.

OTHER THINGS TO TRY

- Suspend a sweet potato (from a home garden; those in supermarkets are treated so they won't sprout) in a jar

of water with three tooth-picks pushed into the flesh. Watch a sweet potato vine grow.

■ Suspend an onion (from a home garden) in a jar of water in the same way. Watch the bulb sprout roots and leaves.

YOU NEED

■ A pineapple
■ A knife and cutting board
■ A 6-inch flower pot
■ Crockery
■ Planting mix, sand, and

coffee grounds
■ Water

TIME OF YEAR

Any time

TIME NEEDED

Several months

PINEAPPLE
___

▲ **Lindsay's mom helps Chris, Sean, Erin, and Karyn cut the top from a pineapple. They will plant it in soil and wait for a pineapple plant to grow.**

GROW A MOLD GARDEN

Plant this garden with your breath, in a "soil" of tomato soup. Watch fantastic growths emerge.

Plant the garden
Put a couple of spoonfuls of tomato soup in the petri dish or jar lid. (Slide the jar lid into the plastic bag.) Blow on the soup. You are planting the garden with spores from your breath! Cover the petri dish or seal the plastic bag. Write the date of planting on a label. Put it on the container.

Watch and record the changes
Make a drawing of your mold garden on planting day and every few days thereafter. In three days to a week, you should see some changes. Look at them through the magnifying glass. Note how the scent of your garden changes, as well. Keep the garden growing for two to four weeks. Isn't it amazing? Make sure that you reseal the container and wash your hands after every observation.

Mold Garden April 29, 1980 Jaime Vachon
Now it looks like I have white fuz on it it looks like your
looking down from a plane on to a farm with black cows.

YOU NEED

- Canned, condensed tomato soup, undiluted
- A spoon
- A petri dish with cover, or a jar lid and zip-closure plastic bag
- A label
- A magnifying glass
- Pencil, crayons or colored pencils, and paper

TIME OF YEAR

Any time

TIME NEEDED

Two to four weeks

MOLD GARDENS

▲ **Justin watches Travis spoon tomato soup into a jar lid. The soup is the "soil" for a mold garden.**

Travis describes his mold garden as it looks two weeks after planting: "My soup is now under the mold. I cannot see any of the soup. I am growing nine types of mold. One looks like a bearskin coat. Another looks like a mouse's fur, and one other looks like mustard with a pinch of ketchup."

WHAT ARE SPORES?

Justin explains, "Spores are very small. They're little germs flying around in air and looking for a place to land."

"There are probably over two million spores in our classroom," Travis continues. "As we breathe, we're breathing them in. They're microscopic. That means you can only see them with a microscope."

MAGICAL MUNCHIES

How do liquids move from the soil to the leaves of a plant? Make magical munchies and find out.

Start the magic

Pour ½-inch of food coloring into the jar. Add an equal amount of water. The more concentrated the color, the more obvious the results will be.

Wash the celery. Cut a bit off the bottom of each stalk. Stand the celery in the colored water.

Watch the magic

In about an hour, some of the bottom leaves should begin to turn the color of the water. How did that happen? Why do the lower leaves turn first? Within a few hours, all the leaves will change color.

Look closely

Cut the celery stalks into 2-inch lengths. Look at one through a magnifying glass. What part of the celery is colored? Pull off a string. What color is it? These "strings" are really tubes that carry food in solution from the soil up to the leaves. Do you think the sap in maple trees runs through tubes like these?

Stuff and eat

Stuff the celery with peanut butter, or cottage cheese and chives. Eat your magical munchies!

YOU NEED

- A few stalks of celery with lots of leaves
- A tall jar
- Red or blue food coloring
- Water
- A knife and cutting board
- A magnifying glass
- Peanut butter, or cottage cheese and chopped chives

TIME OF YEAR

Any time

TIME NEEDED

Several hours

TREVOR: "WOW! Look at that blue! The whole side! It's drinking up the colored water."

SEAN: "Look how much the celery sucked up . . . probably because of the little veins it's got."

DAVID: "Where it's cut you can see the blue tubes. When you eat celery, you know that stringy stuff? That's what's bringing up the blue stuff."

SPREADING

► **(TOP)Karyn fills "striped" celery with cottage cheese.**

EATING

► **(BOTTOM) "Mmmm, Magical Munchies taste yummy!"**

CHAPTER 12

LET'S GROW!
INDOOR EDIBLES

Salad fixin's and kitchen herbs are fun to grow indoors during the winter months. Some crops are ready in a week or less! All you need is good light, either from a window or fluorescent tubes (see p. 48).

▼ **Nothing tastes as good as something you've grown yourself.**

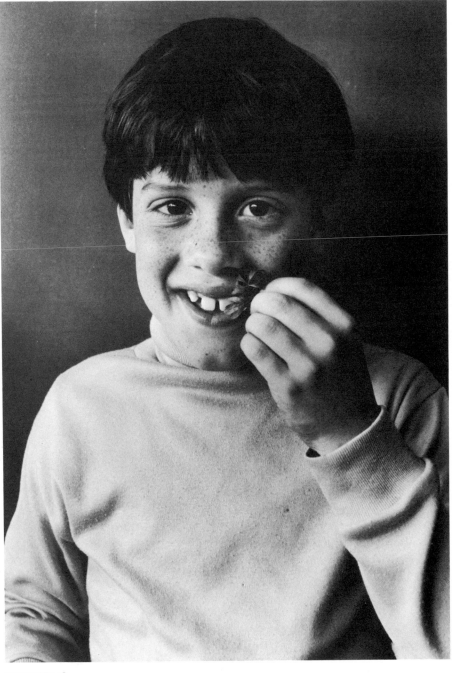

HARVESTING

◄ **Will and Paddy harvest cress with a scissors and prepare to sample its peppery taste.**

SPROUT 'EM!

Now that you know how seeds germinate, sprout some to eat. Sprouting seeds are LOADED with vitamins.

▼ Paddy and Will plant sponge salad.

ON A SPONGE: GROW SPONGE SALAD

No soil is needed for this quick crop of peppery garden cress.

YOU NEED

- Garden cress seeds
- A new sponge
- A shallow dish
- Water and a watering can
- Scissors

TIME OF YEAR

Any time

TIME TO HARVEST

Two weeks

Plant the sponge
Rinse out the new sponge several times with fresh water. Place it in the shallow dish. Sprinkle cress seeds into the depressions in the sponge. Add water to the dish.

Watch it grow
By the very next day, the seed coats will begin to crack. You should see roots by the third day and beginnings of leaves by the fourth. Keep water in the dish so the sponge stays moist.

Harvest and eat
In two weeks or less, you can snip off the cress with scissors. Sprinkle on top of salad or make a cress sandwich. Enjoy the peppery taste.

CHILDREN DESCRIBE THE TASTE OF GARDEN CRESS:

It tastes like steamy, hot fire.

It tastes like Mexican hot peppers.

It tastes like a missile in your mouth.

ON CLAY: GROW A FUR COAT FOR AN ANIMAL

Plant chia seeds in the grooves of a terra-cotta animal and watch a feathery green coat sprout. These hollow sculptures are sold widely on the West Coast, and are available by mail order. If you have clay and access to a kiln, you can make your own.

Soak, soak, soak
Mix a packet of chia seeds with ¼ cup of water. Let soak overnight. Submerge the animal in water, too.

Plant
Spread the seed paste evenly into the grooves of the sculpture. Set the animal in the saucer and fill the planting hole with water. Put your animal in a place with good light, but not direct sun. Keep the planting hole filled with water, and mist the sprouts occasionally. Watch green fur grow!

Harvest and Eat
Snip the sprouts with a scissors and use in the same way as garden cress.

■ NOTE: You can also grow grass seed in this way. Soak the sculpture overnight. Roll it in dry grass seed, covering all the roughed-up surfaces with seed. Care for it as described above.

■ NO SCULPTURE? No problem! Plant on top of a soaked, clean brick instead.

YOU NEED
■ A hollow terra-cotta sculpture, with roughed-up sides and a watering hole on top
■ Chia seeds
■ A saucer
■ Water and a watering can
■ A spray-misting bottle
■ Scissors

TIME OF YEAR
Any time

TIME TO HARVEST
Four to seven days

SPREADING SEEDS
▲ **(TOP) Lindsay spreads a paste of soaked chia seeds on the textured surface of a terra cotta sheep.**

FINISHED
▲ **(BOTTOM) Sprouted chia seeds make lush wool for the sheep.**

YOU NEED
■ Alfalfa seeds
■ A wide-mouth canning jar
■ A plastic sprouting cover or a piece of screen cut to fit inside the outer ring or a piece of cheesecloth and a rubber band
■ Water
■ A pan to put under the jar

TIME OF YEAR
Any time

TIME TO HARVEST
Four or five days

IN A JAR: GROW ALFALFA SPROUTS

Here's a nutritious crop that's fun to grow because you can see everything happen.

Soak the seeds
Make sure you buy seeds that have not been chemically treated. Add a tablespoon of alfalfa seeds to a pint jar, or two tablespoons to a quart jar. Add a half jar of warm water and let soak overnight. In the morning, remove floating seeds. They won't sprout. Put on the cover and pour off water.

Rinse, rinse, rinse
Rinse seeds with warm water and drain. Lay the jar on its side in a pan and put it in a warm closet. Rinse three times a day.

Green-up time
After the seeds have sprouted leaves, put them in indirect sun for a day. Watch the leaves turn green. Then keep them in the refrigerator until you are ready to eat them—if you can wait at all!

Mmmm, good
Munch on raw sprouts, add them to salads, sprinkle them on melted cheese sandwiches. Mix them with scrambled eggs, float them on soup, add them to casseroles. Have fun, and know that while you nibble, you're getting lots of vitamins from this quick 'n' easy crop.

▼ **Jared and friends plant lettuce seeds in a tub. The chicken wire helps them space the seeds.**

GROW A TUB OF LETTUCE

Nibble on homegrown lettuce when winter snows swirl outside.

YOU NEED

- A plastic dishpan
- Pebbles
- Planting mix
- A piece of chicken wire the size of the dishpan (optional)
- Seeds for looseleaf lettuce and radishes
- Water, a watering can, and spray-misting bottle
- Plastic wrap
- Liquid plant food

TIME OF YEAR

Winter

TIME TO HARVEST

Four to six weeks

Plant the lettuce
Put an inch of pebbles in the bottom of the dishpan. Fill it to an inch below the top with moistened planting mix. Lay the chicken wire over the top of the tub and drop a lettuce seed through each hole. Add a radish seed here and there. Lift the chicken wire and sprinkle a very thin blanket of planting mix over the seeds. Spray thoroughly with water, trying not to disturb the tiny seeds.

Wait and watch
Cover the top of the tub with plastic wrap. Watch for the seeds to sprout. Radishes will be first, then lettuce. Can you tell the difference?

Nurture
Remove the plastic wrap, and set the tub in a cool place with good light. Lettuce does not like heat. (Alas, my first graders and I "cooked" our first batch of lettuce in hot sun, when it was almost ready to eat.) Water to keep soil moist, and mist the plants daily. After three weeks, add liquid fertilizer once a week.

Harvest and eat
Harvest radishes when roots are plump, in about four weeks. At the same time, snip off some of the lettuce plants to thin the crop. Use them in a salad or sandwich. After about six weeks, harvest the rest of the lettuce. Just snip it off, wash, and enjoy spring salad in midwinter.

THINNING

▲ **By pulling some of the seedlings, Jared makes sure the others will have plenty of room.**

GROW AN INDOOR HERB GARDEN

Snips of fresh parsley, basil, chives, and thyme surely beat the dried versions. This is easy for a child to grow on a kitchen windowsill.

YOU NEED

- A small plastic window-box or similar container
- Pebbles
- Planting mix
- Herb seedlings:
  2 chives
  2 thyme
  2 parsley
  2 basil
- A small trowel or large spoon
- Water and a watering can
- Liquid fertilizer
- Scissors

TIME OF YEAR

Any time

TIME TO HARVEST

Three weeks, then continuously

INDOOR HERBS

◀ **Meghann firms the soil around the parsley seedlings in her indoor herb garden.**

◀ **Planting plan, Indoor Herb Garden**

Plant the herbs
Put an inch of pebbles in the bottom of the container. Fill it to an inch below the top with moistened planting mix. Using the planting plan as a guide, dig a small hole with the trowel or spoon for each seedling. Set the seedling in the hole at the same depth it was growing. Firm the soil around it. Water well to settle soil around roots.

Care for the herbs
Set the garden on a sunny windowsill or under artificial light (see p. 48). Water when soil seems dry. After three weeks, fertilize weekly with a half-strength solution of liquid fertilizer.

Snip and eat
After about three weeks, snip off herbs to add to salads and sandwiches, and for the chef to add to whatever's cooking. Most kids like to nibble on fresh raw parsley. Now it's only a scissors-snip away!

What next?
If you keep trimming the herbs often, they will keep growing for a long time. If you like, move the herb garden outdoors in summer.

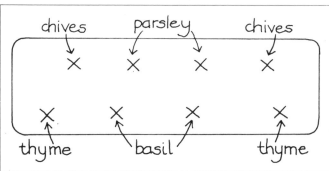

chives   parsley   chives
thyme   basil   thyme

CHAPTER 13

LET'S GROW! HOUSEPLANTS

BABY SPIDER

◀ **Each spider plant baby has its own roots.**

PIGGY-BACK PLANT

▶ **Kathy Link helps Jared break off a baby from a piggy-back plant.**

GROW THREE HOUSEPLANTS THAT HAVE BABIES

Watch babies grow on a spider plant, piggy-back plant, or strawberry geranium, then contribute to a population boom. Root the babies and give them as gifts.

SPIDER PLANT

The spider plant, easiest to grow, sends out long wands as it matures. Delicate, six-petalled white flowers grow along each wand, and at the tip a baby plant forms. The baby looks like a spider dropping on a dragline from the parent plant. Learn its Latin name, *Chlorophytum comosum.*

Care
Spider plants are not fussy. They grow best in filtered sunlight, or will grow less quickly in partial shade. Hang them up and keep them moist, but not sodden. Feed them once a month with liquid fertilizer, except in winter, when they rest. Mist the plant to increase humidity.

PIGGY-BACK PLANT

The piggy-back plant, *Tolmiea menziesii,* is also easy to grow. At the base of each mature leaf a baby plant sprouts, getting a piggy-back ride from its parent. Another name for this plant is Mother-of-Thousands.

Care
The piggy-back plant likes bright light, but not direct sun. Do not spray it with water; hairy-leaved plants don't like that! Keep the soil moist but not sodden. You'll know when you've forgotten to water. The plant will wilt, gasping for a drink. Fertilize once a month, except in winter.

Spider plant

Piggy-back plant

Strawberry geranium

SPIDER PLANT FAMILY

▲ **Young plants drop like spiders on drag lines from the parent spider plant.**

BABY PLANT

▶ **Karyn observes a baby strawberry geranium plantlet at the end of a runner.**

STRAWBERRY GERANIUM

The strawberry geranium (sometimes called strawberry begonia) is neither a geranium nor a begonia. Its Latin name is *Saxifraga.* *S. sarmentosa* and *S. stolonifera* are two varieties. It has scalloped leaves edged with white and pink. Delicate white flowers on thin stalks rise a foot above the plant. The parent sends out long, fragile red runners, and at the end of each runner is a baby plant.

Care
This plant is a bit more fussy. It likes to be in a cool place, below 60°F, with good light, but no direct sunlight. Let the soil get slightly dry between waterings. Fertilize three times a year.

POT UP SOME BABIES

Prepare the pots
Put a piece of crockery over the drainage hole in the bottom of each flower pot. Fill it ⅔ full with moistened planting mix.

Anchor the baby
Snip a baby spider plant or strawberry geranium, with a short piece of runner, off the parent plant. Put it in the flower pot, fill in with soil, and firmly press the soil around the plant.

To plant a baby piggy-back, cut the stem of the parent leaf. Bury the stem and the parent leaf, leaving the baby above the soil.

Use a hairpin to anchor a baby strawberry geranium or piggy-back in the planting mix. Water well.

(If you prefer, don't cut the runner from the parent plant right away. Anchor a spider or strawberry geranium plantlet in a flower pot, water it, and wait until the baby starts to grow on its own before cutting the runner.)

What next?
Keep the planting mix moist but not sodden. Soon the baby will grow roots and begin new top growth. It's a great gift. Or transplant it to a larger pot and wait for grandchildren!

YOU NEED

- A parent plant with babies
- Small flower pots
- Crockery
- Planting mix
- Hairpins
- Water and watering can

TIME OF YEAR

Any time, but the plants will root most quickly in spring

▼ **A baby strawberry geranium develops at the end of each runner.**

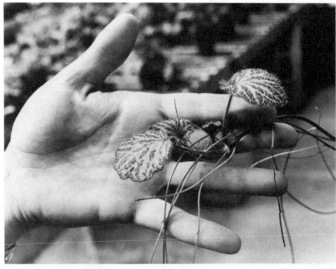

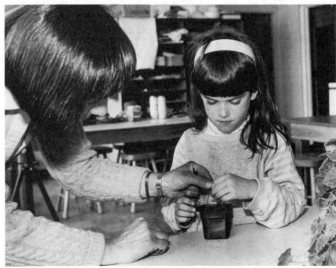

PLANTING

▲ **The author helps Karyn anchor a baby piggy-back plant with a bobby pin.**

PARENT PLANT

◄ **This strawberry geranium produces delicate white flowers on thin stalks. Karyn thinks they're lovely.**

GROW A PLANT THAT LIVES ON AIR

It doesn't grow in soil and it doesn't grow in water; it really lives in the air!

In the jungles of Central America, tillandsias anchor themselves on the bark of trees, but they are not parasites. They are "epiphytic," gathering nutrients from rain and dust in the air. (The Spanish moss that hangs on trees in the South is a cousin.) A child can keep a "pet" tillandsia in a seashell, anchor it to a piece of driftwood, or attach a few to pieces of cork and make a mobile.

Give it a home
Your tillandsia can live in a seashell or on a piece of driftwood. Leave it loose in the shell or anchor it with a drop or two of glue. Attach the root to a pocket in the driftwood with a bit of glue. Hold it until the glue sets. Drape a little sphagnum moss around the base of the plant.

Give it loving care
Give your plant a name and talk to it every day. Keep it in filtered sunlight. Mist it with water once or twice a week, depending on how dry the air is. Or submerge it in water overnight once every other week. Add plant food to water once a month in spring and summer. Do not let its roots and base sit in water or soil. It needs good air circulation. Always keep it where the temperature is above 45°F.

What next?
If the plant is happy, it may flower. Then it will send out "pups" to take its place, and it will die. Now you have a family of tillandsias. Leave them where they are, or mount each pup on a piece of cork and build a tillandsia mobile. Suspend each piece of cork from a length of nylon fishing line and hang them from a coat hanger or a dowel.

YOU NEED
- A tillandsia plant
- A spray-misting bottle
- Water and liquid plant food
- A seashell, or a piece of driftwood, sphagnum moss, and non-toxic glue

TIME OF YEAR
Any time

PET PLANT

▲ **Jamie and Chris have a pet plant. It can live in a shell, without soil.**

CLOSEUP

◄ **Tillandsias, like other air plants, gather nutrients from rain and dust in the air.**

GROW FLOWERING BULBS INDOORS

PAPERWHITE

▲ **Ny adds water to come to the base of the paperwhite bulb he has planted on top of pebbles.**

YOU NEED

- Paperwhite bulbs
- A container twice as deep as the bulbs
- Pebbles
- Water and a watering can

TIME OF YEAR

Late fall and winter

TIME NEEDED

Four to six weeks

PAPERWHITES

Fragrant paperwhites bring a promise of spring to bleak midwinter. Water them and they will grow—perfect for a child's project. In China, it's traditional to have paperwhites in bloom for the New Year celebration.

Pot them
Fill the container ⅔ full with pebbles, and place the bulbs on top of them—as many as will fit. Add water up to the base of the bulbs. Put more pebbles over and around the bulbs to hold them down. Make sure the tips are above the pebbles.

Darkness first
Paperwhites will have a chance to grow sturdy root systems if you put them in a cool, dark place for about two weeks. Then bring them into the light and watch leaves and stems develop quickly. They really don't like heat. Try to find a sunny spot that stays below 60°F. Never put them near the wood stove or fireplace! Keep water up to the base of the bulb. Watch close up as the flower bud swells. What day will it open? Will it be out in time for Christmas? Or for your birthday? When the flowers bloom, enjoy this breath of spring indoors.

AMARYLLIS

Amaryllis is an indoor giant, with flowers six to eight inches across in reds, pinks, and oranges. It is a native of South Africa.

Plant and water
Put a piece of crockery over the hole in the flower pot. Add planting mix and set the bulb so its top is above the soil level. Press the planting mix firmly around the bulb. Water well. Put in a sunny, warm spot and watch it grow, watering daily after the bud appears. (NOTE: Amaryllis often comes prepotted. Just water and let it grow!)

What next?
If you want to save your bulb for another year, fertilize it monthly as it grows. After it blooms, cut off the flower head. The stalk and leaves will build strength for next year's bloom. You can set the plant, pot and all, in the garden after all danger of frost is past. Continue to water and fertilize until the leaves turn yellow. Then cut off the foliage 1 inch above the bulb's "nose" and stop watering. Store in a cool, dry place and do not water until you are ready to start again. Amaryllis roots don't like to be disturbed, so instead of repotting, put some dehydrated cow manure on the surface of the soil (this is called top-dressing) when you start watering again.

SOMETHING ELSE TO TRY

Buy a hyacinth bulb and a hyacinth glass. Put the bulb in the glass; add water to the base of the bulb. Put it on the back shelf of the refrigerator until the glass is filled with roots. Then move it to a cool but sunny windowsill. Keep water up to the base of the bulb and turn it every day to keep the stalk straight. Inhale the lovely fragrance as the hyacinth blooms!

YOU NEED

- An amaryllis bulb
- A flower pot 1 inch wider than the bulb
- Crockery
- Planting mix
- Water and a watering can

TIME OF YEAR

Fall and winter

TIME NEEDED

Six to eight weeks

MAGNIFICENT

▲ **(TOP) Mike and his mom admire their amaryllis.**

GIANT

▲ **An amaryllis flower is 6 to 8 inches across!**

GLOSSARY

ANTHER.
A small pollen-producing sac at the top of the stamen of a flower.

CAMBIUM.
A very thin layer of cells just inside the bark of a woody plant, where growth takes place. Cambium is the green layer you find if you scrape off the outer bark of a twig.

COMPOSITE.
A flower that is actually a cluster of small flowers (florets) contained in one head. Sunflowers and dandelions are composites.

COTYLEDON.
The "seed leaf" of a plant, contained within the seed, and emerging as the first leaf (or leaves) when the seed germinates. In some plants, such as beans, the cotyledons contain stored food for the plant to use when it begins to grow. In other plants, the food is stored in a different part of the seed.

CROWN.
The point at which the root of a plant joins the stem.

DAMPING-OFF FUNGUS.
A fungus that lives in soil and causes young seedlings to wilt and rot at the soil line.

EPIPHYTIC.
Getting its nutrients from rain and dust in the air. Epiphytic plants often anchor themselves to the bark of trees.

FLORET.
One of the small flowers that cluster together in the head of a composite flower.

FRUIT.
The mature, ripened ovary of a flower.

GERMINATION.
The point at which a seed begins to grow. Germination times vary with the type of seed.

GREEN MANURE.
A crop which is dug into the soil to provide nutrients for soil enrichment. A green manure is sometimes called a cover crop.

HARDENING OFF.
The process of letting a plant which has been started indoors become gradually accustomed to being outdoors before it is planted in the garden.

LEADER.
The topmost, central growing tip of an evergreen tree.

NITROGEN-FIXING BACTERIA.
Bacteria found in the soil and in the root nodules of peas, beans, and other legumes. They have the ability to take nitrogen from the air and convert it to nitrogen compounds that plants can use.

NODULES.
Little lumps on the roots of peas, beans, and other legumes. Inside these nodules are nitrogen-fixing bacteria.

OVARY.
The part of a flower in which seeds are formed.

OVULES.
The female cells of a flower that will become seeds after they are fertilized by the male cells contained in pollen.

PETRI DISH.
A shallow, circular glass or plastic dish with a cover, used in science experiments.

pH.
A measure of the acidity or alkalinity of a substance, such as soil or water. On a scale of 0 to 14, 0 is very acidic, 14 is very alkaline, and 7 is neutral. Most plants grow best in soil that is neutral or slightly acidic.

PISTIL.
The female part of a flower, consisting of the stigma, style, and ovary.

POLLINATE.
To cause pollen from a flower to fall on the stigma of the same or another flower. Then a pollen tube grows down through the style to the ovary, where a male cell in the pollen will fertilize the ovule. Wind, insects, and birds help to pollinate flowers.

SEED COAT.
The hard outer covering of a seed.

STAMEN.
The male part of a flower, consisting of the anther and filament.

STIGMA.
The top surface of the pistil of a flower, which receives the pollen.

TOP DRESSING.
An application of manure, compost, or the like to the surface of the soil, either in the garden or in a container, usually after plants are growing.

RESOURCES

TOOLS

Plow & Hearth
560 Main St.
Madison, VA 22727

Carries the tools used by the children in this book.

Smith & Hawken
25 Corte Madera
Mill Valley, CA 94941

Carries children's fork, spade, rake, seed collections, children's gloves, gardening T-shirts.

PUBLICATIONS

Your Big Backyard
(preschoolers)
Ranger Rick (ages 6 to 12)
National Wildlife Federation
1412 Sixteenth St., N.W.
Washington, DC 20036-2266

Both monthly magazines teach children about the wonders of the natural world.

PROGRAMS

Children's Garden Program
Brooklyn Botanic Garden
1000 Washington Ave.
Brooklyn, NY 11225

Begun in 1914, this is the model for such programs. For a minimal fee, children work together to prepare, plant, tend, and harvest their own small plots. The Brooklyn Botanic Garden also produces a video package, with "Get Ready, Get Set, Grow!", a 15-minute video for children ages 9 to 14, a how-to booklet, and an adult's handbook.

*National Gardening
Association*
180 Flynn Ave.
Burlington, VT 05401

National clearinghouse of information on youth gardening. Creator of GROW LAB, an 8-foot-square indoor gardening center, designed for classroom use, where children can grow plants from seed to maturity in less than three months. Awards Gardening Grants—100 grants every year to youth groups with outdoor gardening programs.

Mrs. Harold G. Williams
Junior Gardeners Chairman
*National Council of State
Garden Clubs*
205 Cobil Drive
Water Valley, MS 38965

Write for information on junior garden clubs.

KITS

Discovery Corner
Lawrence Hall of Science
University of California
Berkeley, CA 94720

Carries Super Sunprint Kit and indoor SOF-POT herb garden kit.

Clyde Robin Seed Co.
P.O. Box 57043
Hayward, CA 94545

Carries A Child's Garden, with seeds, stakes, string, and how-to booklet.

Mellinger's, Inc.
2310 W. South Range Rd.
North Lima, OH 44452

Carries Kinder-Garden, with seeds and black plastic pre-printed with illustrations.

W. Atlee Burpee Co.
300 Park Ave.
Warminster, PA 18974

Carries Kinder-Garden (see above) with seed packets, stakes, and how-to booklet.

CIDERMAKING EQUIPMENT

Jaffrey Cider Press
P.O. Box 226
Mount Vernon, NH 03057

Happy Valley Ranch
Route 2, Box 83
Paola, KS 66071

POTPOURRI SUPPLIES

Aphrodisia
282 Bleeker St.
New York, NY 10014

Tom Thumb Workshops
P.O. Box 322
Chincoteague, VA 23336

Caswell-Massey
111 8th Ave. Room 723
New York, NY 10011

Indiana Botanic Gardens
P.O. Box 5
Hammond, IN 46325

INDEX